Jesus and his Relationships

GW00401649

TEAM VARIETY 32

OTHER EASNEYE LECTURES PUBLISHED BY
PATERNOSTER PRESS

1996   Colin Chapman
        Islam and the West: Conflict,
        Co-existence or Conversion?
        (published in 1998)

Jesus and his Relationships

Martin Goldsmith

Authentic
LIFESTYLE

Copyright © 2000 Martin Goldsmith

First published in 2000 by Paternoster Press
Reprinted 2002

08 07 06 05 04 03 02 8 7 6 5 4 3 2

Paternoster Press is an imprint of Authentic Media,
P.O. Box 300, Carlisle, Cumbria, CA3 0QS, UK
and PO Box 1047, Waynesboro, GA 30830-2047, USA
Website: www.paternoster-publishing.com

The right of Martin Goldsmith to be identified as the Author of this
Work has been asserted by him in accordance with the Copyright,
Designs and Patents Act 1988.

*All rights reserved. No part of this publication may be reproduced,
stored in a retrieval system, or transmitted in any form or by any
means, electronic, mechanical, photocopying, recording or otherwise,
without the prior permission of the publisher or a licence permitting
restricted copying. In the UK such licences are issued by the Copyright
Licensing Agency, 90 Tottenham Court Road, London W1P 9HE.*

British Library Cataloguing in Publication Data
A catalogue record for this book is available from the British Library

ISBN 1-84227-028-1

Unless otherwise stated, Scripture quotations are taken from the
HOLY BIBLE, NEW INTERNATIONAL VERSION
Copyright © 1973, 1978, 1984 by the International Bible Society.
Used by permission of Hodder and Stoughton Limited. All rights
reserved. 'NIV' is a registered trademark of the International Bible
Society. UK trademark number 1448790

Cover Design by Mainstream, Lancaster
Typeset by WestKey Ltd, Falmouth, Cornwall
Printed in Great Britain by
Cox & Wyman Ltd, Reading, Berkshire

Contents

Series Preface

Easneye is the name of a small hill on the edge of the river Lea, twenty-five miles north of London between the town of Ware and the village of Stanstead Abbotts in Hertfordshire, England. It was purchased in 1867 by the son of Sir Thomas Fowell Buxton, 'The Liberator', who had been responsible, with William Wilberforce, for the abolition of the slave trade. The beautiful house portrayed on the back cover was completed in 1869 and remained the home of the Buxton family and the hub of their broad missionary and philanthropic involvements for several generations.

Since 1971 Easneye has been the home of **All Nations Christian College** which, since its foundation in 1923, has been training people for cross-cultural Christian mission – people who continue to come from all over the world and go to the ends of the earth for the sake of the gospel.

The Easneye Lectures are delivered as an annual series at All Nations by a visiting guest lecturer who is noted in the field of missiology. The purpose of the Lectures is to enhance the level of theological reflection on the practice of mission, to explore the riches of mission history throughout the world, and to contribute to current debates surrounding missiological issues and challenges.

Lady Hannah Buxton, widow of Sir Thomas, in a letter written to her grandson on 8 May 1869, expressed this prayer for the fine building at Easneye:

> That it may ever be inhabited by faithful servants of God in and through Christ Jesus, and that it may ever be a habitation of God in the hearts of the inhabitants by the Holy Spirit, and Christ be honoured, confessed and served, and this place be a fountain of blessing in the church and in the world.

This vision constantly inspires those who live, work and study at All Nations, and the **Easneye Lectures** are prepared and published in the same spirit.

Chris Wright

Introduction

In the past few years I have observed the immediate interest which talk about Jesus' relationships arouses. From time to time when speaking at a church or university Christian Union I have commented that as Christians we should be studying and modelling our lives and the life of the church on Jesus' relationships – with the Father and the Holy Spirit within the eternal Trinity; with his followers, disciples and friends; with the crowds, the poor, the marginalized and the disabled; with men, women and children; with his opponents and enemies, political and religious leaders; with his own fellow Jews, Samaritans and Gentiles. This approach to the study of Jesus Christ and to our discipleship of him has noticeably struck a vital chord in people.

As Protestant Christians we have always believed that we are under Scripture and only secondarily under tradition as our authority. But then, I confess that for nearly the whole of my Christian life I have just accepted tradition on the question of Christology – the doctrine of the person of Christ. I have just assumed along with our Protestant, or our Christian, tradition over the centuries, that the study of Jesus Christ should be divided into study of the person of Christ and the work of Christ. How else could we understand Jesus? But in more recent years I have realized increasingly the importance of the relationships of

Christ – not only in his life on earth but also in his life eternally in heaven. These relationships are in themselves revelatory.

For some years now I have been challenging people to look at Jesus Christ through the lens of his relationships and to use his relationships as the basis for understanding God, the Christian life, mission and the life of the church. But I have always thought that other people would do the hard work of actually researching the subject! And then when I was asked to do these lectures, rashly and unwisely I agreed to speak on the topic of the relationships of Christ.

I am aware of the danger of being bound by traditional understandings of Christ related to the early church's battles over how three can be one, and one can be three. We may also become defensive in reaction to the Muslim accusation against Christians that we are weak on mathematics, because we say that one plus one plus one equals one. Likewise they question how Jesus can be 100 per cent divine and 100 per cent human and yet still be only 100 per cent. The early church in its study of Christology struggled with such issues. These issues are still important for us today as we communicate the gospel in the context of non-trinitarian monotheistic faiths, particularly Islam and Judaism. But I believe we need to go beyond and break out of the shackles of that traditional Christology to look at the relationships of Christ more seriously. And I hope that these introductory ventures into this large topic may not only be a help to us, but that they also may play a small part in stimulating others more competent than myself to develop this area of Christology more fully. May this book challenge and encourage those who read it to model their relationships on those of Christ.

Existential postmodernism

We need to study Jesus' relationships for two reasons. Firstly, Jesus Christ's relationships are important because of the contemporary postmodern focus on relationships in an age of reaction against impersonal structures, institutionalism and loneliness. It is interesting that, in recent surveys of students in tertiary education in both the European Union and Britain over 90 per cent of the respondents said that their number one problem in life was loneliness. I think this rather surprised some more politically-minded people, who thought it would be student finances, or students' studies, or their accommodation which would be the big problem. But it was not so; the number one problem was actually related to relationships – namely loneliness. In the postmodern world relationships are under stress; people in the postmodern world may not know how to handle it, so life in our world continues to be lonely and relationships weak. The postmodern world tends to be individualistic and society is fractured. But we as Christians are called to speak into this postmodern situation. The relationships of Christ as a model for us in our relationships surely speak to us today.

Secondly, Jesus' relationships are important because theology has always traditionally been rooted in mission, in the actual needs of people. This has been true from New Testament times. When we study such great christological passages as Colossians 1:15–20 or Philippians 2:5–11, we notice that they stem from particular experiences in situations of everyday life. So in Philippians 2 the context is that we should have the mind of Christ, with relationships of unselfish love and humility. Why does Paul feel he needs to emphasize this Christ-like attitude? It is evident from Philippians 4:2 that there were in the church two women

who disagreed (we don't want to be sexist in our understanding of this verse; it could equally well have been two
men, but it happened in this case to be two women). This
quarrel represented a vital need in the church; you *cannot*
have a church, a living church, if there are two people in it
who are in serious disagreement. This damns the whole life
and mission of the church. The life of the Christian church
and the good news we proclaim are centred on the great
truths of love, reconciliation and forgiveness. Unreconciled
quarrels between Christians are an evident denial of the
gospel.

Not only Paul's theology, but also that of the early
church, was always rooted in mission and contemporary
apologetics. It was not formed in an ivory tower. Academic
theology unrelated to the needs of people and to specific
situations is a more recent development and introduces a
weakness into the whole practice of theology. So
Christology, our understanding of Jesus Christ, must be
looked at in the context of mission today – and mission
today is increasingly in a postmodern context where
relationships are important. Therefore I believe this subject
of Jesus' relationships is vital for us in God's church and in
our mission.

Objective revelation

Our theme in this book relates not only to the existential
situation of postmodernism and to the ideal of a theology
rooted in relevant reality, but also, thirdly, to the fact that
Jesus' relationships are an essential element in his calling.
This was to reveal the nature of God and to be the model for
the life of the church as a body and for each one of us individually as his followers. Of course this relates also to the
mission to which God calls us as his people.

It is encouraging to see that one or two theologians have begun to explore this subject. In Cunningham's *These Three are One* (Blackwell, 1998), he has dedicated one small section of this book on the Trinity to the relationships within the Trinity. Students at All Nations Christian College, for example, have been encouraged to read Witherington's book on the Christology of Jesus (Fortress Press, 1990). But Witherington still tends to use the relationships of Christ merely as a means to study the traditional theological truths of the person and work of Christ, rather than to see the relationships as in themselves of significance in God's revelation. In these Easneye lectures we want to underline that Jesus' relationships are in themselves significant – not just as supporting evidence for other theological truths.

Clearly, as Christian disciples and as Christian missionaries, we are called to follow Jesus Christ. The call of Jesus to his disciples was always, 'Follow me!' Discipleship involves being like him, in his image. Indeed we are to become increasingly like him, being recreated according to the image of our creator (Col. 3:10). That process of being recreated according to the image of our creator is not only in personal morality and holiness, nor even only in the structural relationships of social justice; it must be also in our interpersonal relationships at the micro level as well as the macro level. Christ's relationships are to be the model of our Christian life, of the churches that we form, and therefore also of our mission.

It was with this background that I chose the topic of the relationships of Christ when invited to give the Easneye Lectures at All Nations Christian College in June 1998 – and it is those lectures which form the basis for this book. Having served as a full-time lecturer at ANCC for 24 years, it is always a particular pleasure and privilege to give some lectures at the college. As Associate Lecturer I have the joy of giving one lecture course each year which also allows close contact with students. My wife and I are deeply grateful for the continued friendship and fellowship we enjoy with members of staff, but we miss the regular inter-action with the college students. I want therefore to thank Dr Chris Wright, the Principal, for doing me the honour of graciously inviting me to deliver the 1998 Easneye Lectures and for the warm welcome he and all the staff have given us. And now I thank Christine King for her unstinting secretarial work in extensive retyping of my lectures in order to bring them into a more literary style – her amazing patience and ability prove that the day of miracles is not over.

1

Relationships within the Trinity

We begin our study with Jesus Christ's relationships within the Trinity. I remember on one occasion being asked to speak at a lively meeting of dynamic young people. After I had spoken they wanted a time of questions, and the leader immediately set the ball rolling. 'What do you feel is the heart of the Christian life?' he asked. Without hesitation I gave him what was to me the obvious reply, 'The Trinity'. The young people showed their surprise by the expression on their faces. I explained how everything in the Christian faith and life ultimately depends on the Trinity.

Sadly, in many of our churches the wonder of the Trinity has been obscured by an arid theological debate based on Greek philosophical concepts which are largely alien to the debates of our day and to contemporary thought patterns. This is tragic because the Trinity presents us with the glorious reality of a God who is on high in the burning splendour of his glory and yet is also intimately with us. In the second person of the Trinity we are united with God himself in an eternal union, so that we are not only crucified with Christ and raised with him to a new life – we are also ascended with him, so that we are seated with him in the heavenlies and our citizenship is now in heaven. And yet we still remain for a while in the realities of a fallen life on earth. Gloriously, God the Holy Spirit is with us and even in us here on earth. If God were not in Trinity, none of this would be possible.

Of course the mystery of Almighty God's essential nature in Trinity remains above and beyond our human comprehension. We would not want our God to be so limited that we could grasp the fullness of his being. By definition God must be infinitely beyond us. We bow before him in awe-filled humility. In this chapter we shall attempt to see just a little glimpse of the wonder of Christ's relationships with the Father and the Spirit within the Trinity.

Separate identity

We notice first of all the reality of the fact that each of the three persons of the Trinity has a separate identity, and yet they live together in unity. They are one, and there is a deep inter-relational harmony. Each person is distinct: the Father is not the Son; and the Son is not the Spirit; and the Spirit is not the Father. And yet despite their separate identities there remains an absolute *shalom*, an absolute harmony and absolute oneness among them.

This truth of separate identity and yet oneness, unity and harmony was emphasized in the development of black theology in the 1970s. There was a seminal anthology called *Black Theology*, edited by Basil Moore. Its subtitle was 'Black Theology with a South African Voice'. In one of the articles in that book an African theologian called Mpunzi says that 'freedom is the key concept in the Christian faith' and he quotes from Galatians 5 in which Paul says 'It is for freedom that Christ has set us free. Stand firm, then, and do not let yourselves be burdened again by a yoke of slavery.' We may imagine, in the apartheid context of South Africa at that time, and in black theology, the significance and impact of a verse like that. Mpunzi sees this freedom in the context of relationships modelled on the Trinity. He emphasizes that in talking of the Trinity 'we do not talk about a God out there, but it is talk about the ultimate in human relationships'. He means that the three persons of the Trinity are uniquely themselves. Mpunzi says, in nice simple English, 'they are who they are'. They are not the other and they are not called to become the other. The Father is the Father and remains the Father. The Son is the Son and remains the Son. The Spirit is the Spirit and remains the Spirit. They are who they are. And so Mpunzi continues: 'Their uniqueness grows out of and is expressed in their unity'. From this he draws the lesson that we, too, are to be uniquely ourselves in our identity, different from others and yet totally at one.

Our knowledge and understanding of African approaches and black theology alerts us to the relevance of the Trinity to the Negritude movement, 'black is beautiful'. 'We are not wanting to become little whites', said Gayroad Wilmore, who coined the pejorative term 'whitenization' – the idea that blacks should become little whites and model themselves on the life, the society, the culture, the relationships and everything else that pertains to whites. They would thus become little whites with black skins. Negritude and black theology stand in direct opposition to that sort of approach. They therefore stress that black is beautiful. All of us are ourselves and we are to remain ourselves, and yet we are to be in harmony together with others who remain *themselves*.

This concept of a unique identity is going to be very important for mission. As a Jewish Christian I know it from my cultural point of view. It is rather assumed that if you are a Jew and you become a Christian then you become a little Gentile. This is seen even in the way one is often introduced in meetings. Again and again I am introduced in this way: 'It's lovely to have Martin here', (they are always polite!) and then they add, 'Martin comes from a Jewish background'. They don't feel quite free to say 'Martin is a Jew', or 'Martin is Jewish'. The statement that you come from a Jewish background assumes that you aren't *really* Jewish any more. This may be contrasted with introductions of ethnic British Christian speakers. No one will say that they come from a British background. This is equally true of other races. Nobody will introduce us as coming from a 'Korean or Chinese background'. If it's relevant they will say we come from Korea or that we are a Korean, but they will not say 'a Korean background' on the assumption that you have become something different.

That is precisely what Mpunzi is standing against. All of us are what we are and we remain what we are. That is vitally important in the whole question of Christian mission – that we are not to 'go *goy*' (go Gentile) as Jewish people say. African and Asian Christians are to remain what they are; they are not to be westernized. We are to be who we are and yet in harmony and unity, not divided. The combination of separate identity with unity relates to the whole question of developing separate churches for different cultures – young people's churches, older people's churches, churches for culturally contemporary or for traditional people, black churches, Jewish churches, etc. With such churches there is a danger of negating the harmony and unity which the Trinity exemplifies. If we are in separate churches, we need to give serious consideration to the question of demonstrating our harmony and unity alongside of our structural separateness. This also relates to the hotly-debated question of contextualized churches as in some Muslim lands like Pakistan, Bangladesh, Malaysia or Indonesia. The worship, preaching and leadership forms of many national churches in these countries are sometimes felt to be unrelated to the culture and religion of Muslims. The question arises, therefore, whether churches should be planted which conform more closely to one particular background. Would such

churches be so separate from other churches that they
would cause disunity?

But in relating together as people of distinct cultures,
each person will have to decide how much they feel it right
to adapt to others in order to reflect the harmony which is
found in the Trinity. Such adaptation may be seen by some
as undesirable compromise and denial of one's own background, while others may applaud it. Thus there is no need
for Jewish believers to 'go *goy*', to become Gentile, or likewise for blacks to become whitenized. To 'go *goy*' is
actually a negative expression. Jews use it to describe something that is very definitely undesirable. To 'go *goy*' is an
accusation. But there is actually a positive word for it,
namely 'assimilation', which is also used. For example, as a
Jewish Christian I am happy to accept that I am assimilated
in the English culture – though I am Jewish I speak good
English, can move in English circles very easily and can be
mistaken for an ordinary English person. But if another Jew
were to say to me that I had gone *goy*, I might object because
it is pejorative. And yet actually the two words
fundamentally mean the same thing. There can, therefore,
be a positive dimension to cultural adaptation. The church
of God is a visible ikon of God in Trinity with the three
distinct persons in complete unity. We are to model ourselves on the relationships in the Trinity in maintaining
both identity and harmony.

Intimate unity

So we are reminded that the three persons of the Trinity are
not only separate persons. In fact it is often not easy in the
New Testament to discern which person one is actually
referring to or relating to. The New Testament sometimes
slips very easily from the Father to the Son or the Son to the

Spirit, or the Spirit to the Son. It begins to talk about one person and suddenly we find it is referring to another person of the Trinity. Because they are so intimately interrelated in their oneness it is very easy to slip from one to the other.

In popular Christian thought, although not of course in more careful theological work, the Father is often described as the creator and the Son as the saviour and the Holy Spirit as the sanctifier. Such descriptions help us to distinguish them, but the New Testament does not allow such over-simplified statements. In actual fact the Son and the Holy Spirit are involved in creation just as much as the Father. And it is not only the Son who saves, but the Father and the Spirit also save; and it is not only the Holy Spirit who is our sanctification, but also the Father and the Son. Although we often talk as if each of the three persons has a separate function, in the New Testament this is patently not so. We cannot separate the persons simply by their functions. For example John 1 and Colossians 1 show the Son as creator; in 1 Corinthians 1:30 Jesus is described as our sanctification; and in 2 Corinthians 1:3 and 4 the Father is the comforter, the paraclete – the same word as is used of the Holy Spirit in John 14. And in Ephesians 4:6 it is the Father who is above, through and in all, but in Colossians 1:17 and 18 it is in Jesus Christ, not in the Father, that all things hold together, that in all things *he* might be pre-eminent. So, is it the Father or the Son who is above all? The three persons actually interrelate so closely that they almost merge in their functions. It is not so easy to define the distinction between them.

So there is a positive example for us in the relationships of the Trinity. We have said that each person of the Trinity is an individual, and yet at the same time they all interrelate in harmony and unity of function. This gives us a basis for the fact that we are actually to relate to each other and to harmonize our lives with one another. Acts 15 gives us an example. What do we do when a large number of Gentiles comes into a Jewish church? How do we integrate them into the church? How do the Jewish Christians relate to the Gentile Christians?

There are many parallel problems in mission today. The Seventh Day Adventists provide us with an example from their history in Britain. Some years ago there were about 10,000 Seventh Day Adventists in Britain – 10,000 'nice' traditional English whites. Then a massive influx of black Afro-Caribbean members arrived, many of whom were already Christians leaders, some of them already pastors. These newcomers took over many of the white churches and some of the 'nice' traditional white churches suddenly found themselves with a black pastor, black music, black forms of Bible teaching and a black culture. About 50 per cent of the white members left. Such radical change was more than they could adjust to. A similar reaction might occur if a young people's, very 'with it' church suddenly had an influx of a few hundred over-80s. This would lead to a demand for considerable changes in the Bible teaching, worship and forms of fellowship. It could also happen the other way round – a church with a congregation of over 80s accustomed to a traditional style might see an influx of long-haired young people, with earrings all along their ears, into their noses and their bellies. The whole style of the church would have to be turned upside down. Coming from the village church of Stanstead Abbotts, I could imagine that there would be one or two in our congregation who would not survive such a change. That is precisely what happened in the New Testament time when a crowd of Gentiles came into a 'nice' Jewish church – and we have had problems ever since.

That is the context in which the New Testament church grappled with the relationships of Jesus within the Trinity and the radical distinction between the Father, the Son and the Spirit. It is in such a context that we observe how the persons of the Trinity are themselves and yet also interrelate intimately, so intimately that they actually harmonize together.

Romans 14 and 15 and Colossians may take on new meaning when seen from the point of view of mixed churches struggling with how Jewish and Gentile Christians should relate together in loving harmony, but without either losing their cultural identity. Some flexibility and compromise will be required in churches where members come from different generations or cultural or ethnic backgrounds. So we, like missionaries, need to practise identification and acculturation or adaptation. When such words are used, we think of a missionary going to another country and contextualized church planting. But we cannot distance ourselves in this way, for such adaptation is necessary for every Christian, modelled on the life of Jesus within the Trinity. Based on the relationships of Jesus, all of us are to adapt to people of different cultures and backgrounds within the church of God. That is likely to prove an ongoing process.

But we also have to ask what these truths of the relationships within the Trinity mean for the mission strategy of today, in relation to the theories and practices of the homogeneous unit principle and the modern emphasis on unreached peoples. There are obvious pragmatic advantages in following the church growth policy that people should not be hindered in their coming to faith in Christ by mere cultural barriers. Jesus and his cross should be the only stumbling block to the gospel. Therefore such movements stress that each ethnic group should have a church of its own people and culture. There is, however, a dangerous weakness in this approach. Separate identity may not be matched by a clear model of unity and harmony. Thus one

aspect of the interpersonal relationships within the Trinity
often prevails to the exclusion of the other – that is, distinc-
tions are emphasized to the detriment of harmony. The
church needs to demonstrate the essential nature of God
both in the reality of separate identity and in the loving
harmony of mutual conformity.

So we have to look again at the interrelationship of the
separate identity and unity within the Trinity. How do the
three persons interrelate, how does diversity co-exist with
some degree of mutual conformity? These are vital issues
for the life of the church in mission in Britain and every
other part of the world.

Image of the invisible God

Jesus Christ in his relationship to the Father is described in
Colossians 1 as the image of the invisible God. In Christ
Jesus the invisible becomes visible, the indescribable
becomes describable. It is interesting that in every religion
this issue of whether God is visible, knowable and describable is to be found. In overseas mission today there is a new
interest in the Orthodox Church because of increasing
mission activity both in the Middle East and in the former
Soviet Union and eastern Europe. Traditionally, western
theology has paid scant regard to the Eastern Church.
Indeed, even today most western theological books and
university theology courses will study the various theologians and theological schools of Roman Catholicism and
Protestantism, but they will not mention Eastern Orthodox
theology or theologians.

For many centuries, Orthodox Christians have struggled
with cataphatic and apophatic theology: whether God is
knowable or unknowable. In response to the extreme
apophatic theology of the fourteenth-century theologian

Barlaam – who said that God is unknowable – great theologians like Gregory Palamas defined a theological position which balances the two extremes. Gregory Palamas emphasized that the indescribable glory of the essence of God can nevertheless be known through the activities of God, which form a ladder to the numinous. Jesus said something similar about the Holy Spirit – that he may be discerned by his moving, like the wind in the trees (Jn. 3:8).

In Islam, too, there is a struggle. The fundamental view of God prevails that he is *akbar* (greater than anything else). As al-Ghazzali maintained, he is only describable in negatives. Yet in Islam God is 'nearer to me than the artery in the neck'; and this cataphatic understanding is stressed by the mystic Sufis. In Judaism too there is a tension in this respect between orthodox Judaism and the more mystical Kabbalists. In Hinduism, the basic description of Brahman is that he is 'neti, neti', not this and not this. Whatever you say, he is not that. So if you say he is good, he is not good. If you say he is bad, he is not bad. If you say he is personal, he is not personal. If you say he is impersonal, he is not impersonal. Brahman is above and beyond description, he is: not this, not this! Such an apophatic theology is found in each of these religions.

In Christianity we also have the God who is beyond, the invisible God (Col. 1:15), the one who is so glorious that you cannot see him, you cannot know him, you cannot relate to him: he is beyond. He is more glorious than any sunshine; he is the absolutely glorious one, beyond all description, beyond all knowledge. And yet at the same time Jesus Christ is revealed as the image of the invisible God, the image of the one of whom it is said, 'nobody can see God and live'. This is the glory of our trinitarian faith, that the God who is invisible and indescribable is also intimate and close to us.

This combination of the apophatic and the cataphatic will influence the communication of our message, the content and style of our communication, and the forms of church life and worship that we institute in our church planting and practise in our churches. Keeping both the absolute glory and the intimacy of God can prove difficult even for Christians, despite our theology of the Trinity and the relationships within the Trinity. If I may parody it slightly, some Christians hold to a form of Christianity in which God seems to be remote at the far end of the church, probably with a screen in front of him. The congregation is seated in serried rows in front, with God far away – distant and removed. This view of God leads to a high worship that is numinous, praying with eyes shut, probably in a kneeling position. Others follow a more recent ritual which emphasizes the God who is amongst us and very close, the image of God who is incarnate amongst us. Such churches may have informal semi-circular seating arrangements so that all look at each other. The emphasis is on warm-hearted fellowship. It used to be that Christians prayed with hands together and eyes closed to demonstrate the greatness of God and awe-filled worship. Today some pray with their hands in their pockets while walking about to demonstrate that God is close to us, loves us and accepts us just as we are. Both emphases are present in the Trinity; indeed both are needed if we are to model our worship and prayer on the fullness of the Trinity. We believe in the unity of the God who is beyond and the God who is present. We believe in the God who is invisible, but whose image is with us in the person of Jesus Christ.

This balance has tremendous significance for our mission to non-trinitarian monotheists – Judaists and Muslims in particular, because they find it almost impossible to keep the two ideas of God together. Their theology cannot easily hold in tension both the invisible God and the God who is intimately present with us. So they either worship the God who is beyond and great, to whom nobody can relate, or they bring God down to earth with beautiful mystic poetry and spirituality but actually lose the awesome worship of the God who is on high and supremely holy. Judaism faces a similar problem to Islam. In an orthodox synagogue, they worship the God who is on high but remote, whereas in kaballistic Judaism in the pietistic Chassidic communities they relate to a God who is intimate and close, but they may lose sight of the God who is on high. But we as Christians know and worship the image of the invisible, the two in harmony together – the God of gracious love who is with us and the God of glory and burning holiness.

Order and equality

Earlier, we posed the question: is it the Father or the Son who is supreme above all? Scripture reveals that there is an order in the Trinity whereby the Father is supreme as the author of all. In John's gospel Jesus reveals that although he is the Son, eternal and uncreated, yet he is under the Father's direction and only does his will. He stems from the Father, or, to use traditional vocabulary, he is eternally begotten of the Father. The expression 'begotten' presents us with some problems, but it explains a profound divine truth in human vocabulary. There never was a time when the second person of the Trinity was not (e.g. Jn. 1:1, 2). He always was, and yet he comes from the Father (Jn. 8:42). The Father remains the Father of all, the source, the author of all, the unique one; and yet, although the Son comes from the Father, the Son always was. We therefore do not say he was 'born' of the Father, but that he was 'eternally begotten' of the Father.

This concept relates closely to what Muslims say about the Qur'an, because the Qur'an in Islam is also the eternal, uncreated word of God. So in Islam the Qur'an is not eternally begotten of the Father but eternally written of Allah. So Muslims face the same issue as Christians in the origin of God's incarnate word. In Islam there never was a time when the Qur'an was not, and yet Allah alone ultimately is. He is the unique God. So there is a parallel in our theologies which is generally not recognized. Although this parallel exists there is also a contrast. In Islam the eternal uncreated word is a book. In Christianity the eternal uncreated word is a person within the glorious Trinity.

But in Christianity Jesus is under the Father, and yet one and equal with the Father. He does not come to Earth of his own volition, nor to follow his own purposes or desires. He is sent by the Father, and he delights to do the will of the Father and to fulfil his purposes. He brings us into relationship with the Father.

Similarly, in the person of the Holy Spirit, there is a parallel. But in the origin of the Holy Spirit and his relationship to the Father and the Son our theology becomes more controversial. On this question the Western churches, Protestant and Roman Catholic, radically disagree with the Eastern churches. In Western theology, as those of us who regularly recite the creeds will know, the Holy Spirit is said to proceed both from the Father and the Son. In Eastern Orthodoxy (and I believe the Eastern Orthodox are in this point correct), the Holy Spirit proceeds only from the Father. This maintains the ultimate, unique supremacy of the Father and the subordination not only of the Spirit but also of the Son to the Father. This is not the place to debate the origins of the *filioque* 'and the Son' phrase in the Western creed. The Orthodox churches maintain that the creeds were changed under Charlemagne and then confirmed in that change because of the struggles with Orthodox mission among Bulgar people. But actually there seems to be some evidence of an earlier usage of the 'and the Son' in Bede's *History of the English Church*. Bede talks of the Council of Hertford in the 400s when bishops in their deliberations used the *filioque* clause. The *filioque* clause distorts the true order of the Trinity, which maintains of the absolute unique supremacy of the Father over all.

We need to note, however, that the Spirit is sent both by the Father and the Son. He is therefore subordinate to both the Father and the Son, but this order has an interesting paradox within its relationships. Jesus is sent by the Father, does the will of the Father, only speaks and acts with the Father's authority, and only teaches what the Father has taught him (Jn. 8:16–29), doing what pleases the Father. And yet there remains an absolute equality between the persons of the Trinity. Likewise the Holy Spirit proceeds from the Father and is sent by the Father and the Son. He is the agent of the Father in creation and revelation. He does the will of the Father in exalting Jesus Christ, in convicting the world of sin, and in sanctifying and renewing the believer. But the Holy Spirit too shares that same absolute equality within the Trinity.

This order and equality, I believe, is a model for the church. Within the Trinity there is an order, but it is not an authority structure leading to different status. Order and equality go together in the Trinity. In spite of the clear order within the Trinity the three persons share an absolute equality. The balance demonstrated in the model of the three persons of the Trinity in their relationships is very important for the church. It is easy to slip into clericalism where leadership is over-emphasized to the detriment of equality. On the other hand, a leaderless democracy in the church can lead to damaging disorder. The leadership struc-tures and attitudes that we work for in mission overseas or in mission in Britain need to be purposefully following the pattern of the Trinity, and not just cultural forms of leadership or the management structures of secular business. God in Trinity is the model for the church of God.

Humility and service

The relationships between the persons of the Trinity are also relationships of humble service. The Spirit points to Jesus Christ. This is the basic function of the Holy Spirit. It is his task to bring people into a relationship with Jesus Christ, to make Jesus real to us. That is also the purpose of the fruit of the Spirit – to reproduce the life and holiness of Jesus within our lives. Likewise it is the ministry of the gifts of the Spirit to strengthen our relationship with Jesus Christ. Neither the gifts nor the fruit of the Spirit have validity in and of themselves; their function is always to bring us into an ever deeper relationship with Jesus Christ and to glorify him. That means that if we are filled with the Spirit we should be talking much of Christ rather than of the Spirit. Also, the Holy Spirit reminds us of all that Jesus has said and bears witness to Jesus. The Spirit glorifies Jesus. But then, likewise, Jesus glorifies and serves the Father. Jesus is the way to the Father, bringing people into relationship with the Father. He is our mediator and our Saviour. Therefore, if we love Jesus Christ, we shall talk much of the Father and worship the Father, because the function of Jesus is not to glorify himself but to glorify the Father.

Then, amazingly, John's Gospel shows that the Father's purpose is to glorify the Son (Jn. 8:50). At the transfiguration the voice from heaven orders the disciples to listen to Jesus Christ because the Father exalts him as his beloved Son (Mt. 17:5). Paul points out in 1 Corinthians 15:24 that Jesus will deliver the kingdom to God the Father –

eschatologically even the Son is subject to God the Father. So the Father alone will be Lord of all.

So we observe in the Trinity an amazing relationship of humility and service, pointing away from self to glorify the other. The Holy Spirit points to Jesus, Jesus glorifies the Father, the Father glorifies the Son, and finally the Son lays everything at the feet of the Father. What a model for Christian mission! What a model for the life of the church! What a model for the Christian life for each one of us! We think immediately of Jesus' words, 'not what I want, but what you want. Not my will, but your will be done' (Mt. 26:39).

Although these words relate supremely to the crucifixion, they apply right through the life of Jesus and then define the principle by which his followers are to live. It is to be regretted how often in the church expressions using 'I like . . .' such as 'I like this sort of music', 'I like this sort of worship', 'I like this sort of teaching' are heard. A spirit of selfishness easily pervades the church. Actually all of us should be fostering attitudes in ourselves and in others that are based on the relationships of Jesus within the Trinity. We are to be humbly pointing away from ourselves, from our own desires, from our own glory, from our own will. We should be concerned with the desires, and the glory of others. This is the model of the Trinity. We are called to be servants of God and servants of one other, to lift up the Lord and one another. Following this pattern of the relationships of the Trinity would solve many problems in our churches, as also in our personal relationships and mission. It would lead to different attitudes in the relationships between churches, where sometimes we tend to glorify ourselves and criticize others.

For example, charismatic churches may find their identity in not being traditional like other churches; and those other churches can easily find their identity in not being like the charismatics. Anglicans may be proud of their own position and tradition, while Baptists may rejoice that they are not like the Anglicans. These people find their identity and self-esteem not in glorifying and esteeming the other, but actually in glorifying themselves to the neglect and detriment of the other. Self-seeking and a desire to build our own kingdoms often characterize both the churches and mission agencies.

So the relationships of the Trinity are the model for all Christian relationships, including the relationships of leaders with others working with them. In every part of the Christian church and in mission the relationships of the Father, the Son and the Holy Spirit lie at the heart of, and are the key to, the life and mission of the church.

Conclusion

In our sinful society and with our fallen natures it is not easy for us to picture the possibility of God the Trinity having separate identity of persons and yet total unity and harmony. Likewise we cannot imagine the definite order which exists in the Trinity together with equality, humble servanthood and self-sacrificing love. In our corrupt human society order virtually always accompanies the exercise of authority, pride and self-seeking dominance.

But life in the kingdom of God challenges us to a God-like holiness in which we strive for his ideal pattern. It is true that in this fallen world we shall fail to achieve that ideal, but we struggle and aim towards it in the assurance that finally, in the full presence of God, we shall be perfectly like him. His relationships are our ideal model of holiness – God-like holiness not just in personal morality but also in our relationships.

2

Jesus' Relationships with his Followers

Each of us as a Christian faces the challenge to grow in the knowledge of God and in appropriating his grace. Yet the temptation to become stuck in a rut comes to us all. Years ago, my aging father-in-law was no longer able to get out of the house and one day I said to him, 'Daddy, you must miss your church.' 'Not really,' he replied, 'people are very good and visit me, so I get lots of fellowship and friendship.' Then he looked searchingly at me and added, 'You see, I've heard it all before.' He then smiled with his deep-set old man's eyes and with a twinkle he said, 'Many times!' I was profoundly challenged by his words: 'I've heard it all before – many times!' Our God is greater than anything we have apprehended and the Bible is richer than anything we have understood. So we need to grow. We are to grow in love, and therefore also in intimacy of relationship.

The paradox of perfect love

When we consider the relationships of Jesus with his followers, a paradox immediately strikes us: he has perfect love for each one and yet there are gradations of intimacy. In the lists of the twelve disciples in the Gospels it is clear that Peter, James and John have a pre-eminent position.

Jesus singles them out on particularly significant occasions when he only wants those who are specially close to him to be with him. For his glorious transfiguration he leaves the other disciples and takes with him those three chosen friends. Likewise, in the garden of Gethsemane, he chooses these three to share his agonized prayer with him. From among those three special disciples Jesus seems to have enjoyed a particularly close relationship with John, 'the disciple whom Jesus loved'.

Jesus loved all his followers, but the home of Martha, Mary and Lazarus held a special place in his heart. Although it would seem that Jesus knew that Lazarus' death was not the end of the story, Jesus wept at the graveside. Similarly it is evident from the Gospels that Mary Magdalene also shared a particularly close relationship with Jesus – so much so that some sensationalist critics have blasphemously suggested an improper liaison between Jesus and Mary Magdalene. There is absolutely no evidence at all for such an accusation. It is clear, however, that Jesus did relate more closely with some of his followers than others.

Indeed there is a gradation in Jesus' relationships. He was particularly close to the three and very specially with John. Martha, Mary, Lazarus and Mary Magdalene were also in the inner circle of intimate friendship with Jesus. But he also loved the others in that band of the twelve disciples. And then surely he also loved the seventy or seventy-two (Lk. 10:1) and indeed all his followers.

We believe that Jesus was perfect in every way, including in his relationships. He is the perfect image of the God whose very nature is love. The fullness of the God of love is found in Jesus who is the glory of God incarnate. So we may affirm that Jesus' love is totally perfect. And yet we see that he is closer with some of his followers than with others, although his love is perfect for them all. This paradox is important for our relationships as Christians.

When I served as a tutor at All Nations Christian College, sometimes the students in my tutorial group demonstrated an unrealistic impatience. They expected an intimate personal sharing in the first weeks of being together as a group, saying that we should love one another and so be open to each other. But within the totally perfect love of God manifest in Jesus we observe varying levels of closeness with different people. We also shall experience this. In our relationships we shall grow in intimacy and openness; so with different people we shall relate at varying levels of closeness. It is unrealistic and not in accordance with the pattern of Jesus himself to expect that our love for all sisters and brothers will lead to immediate closeness and openness together. Close relationships usually take time to build.

Jesus gave to his disciples the unique privilege of being called his friends. John 15:12–17 says

'My command is this: Love each other as I have loved you. Greater love has no-one than this, that they lay down their lives for their friends. You are my friends if you do what I command. I no longer call you servants, because a servant does not know his master's business. Instead, I have called you friends, for everything that I learned from my Father I have made known to you. You did not choose me, but I chose you to go and bear fruit – fruit that will last. Then the Father will give you whatever you ask in my name. This is my command: Love each other. . . .'

'I have called you friends', Jesus says – not slaves, not servants, but friends. And yet in the New Testament the early Christians humbly gave themselves the title of 'slave'. In his epistles and his letters Paul often starts with 'I, Paul, a slave of Jesus Christ', and he boasts of his position as a slave of Jesus Christ. The New Testament was written and Paul lived in a context where slavery was a fearful reality. It was not just a theory or something remembered from the past; it was a common, living reality which engendered deep bitterness and suffering.

I remember sharing in an inter-racial student conference in South Africa in the heyday of apartheid. In one meeting I purposely said to the students, 'We are called to be slaves.' Horror rippled through the black students present. It was, of course, an unacceptable thing to say. I then pointed out that Paul had said the same in a time when it was equally unacceptable, in a day when slavery was still very common.

We are indeed called to be slaves of Jesus Christ. But from his side in his relationship with us Jesus graciously says that he does not treat us as slaves. He accepts us as his friends. This means that he shares intimately with us.

Our friendship with Jesus not only allows us the inestimable privilege of an intimate relationship with Jesus, but it also carries with it the responsibility of obedience. Indeed obedience is a condition of that friendship – 'You are my friends if you do what I command' (Jn. 15:14). In the gospels there is a strong emphasis on the fact that as followers of Jesus we are to be obedient to him, we are to do the good works that he commands. God commands us to produce the fruit of good works that he expects. Evangelicals are often somewhat shy of emphasizing good works because of the clear biblical teaching that good works are not the means of salvation or justification. So good works may be down-played. But doing good works and producing the fruit of righteousness may demonstrate that we are his disciples. Doing good works stands as a condition of being Jesus' friends. 'You are my friends *if* you do what I command', he declared.

In John 15, friendship with Jesus, and Jesus' friendship with us, is in the context of his self-sacrifice for his disciples.

'Greater love has nobody than this, than that he lay down his life for his friends.' Jesus laid down his life for his friends, for his disciples and also for us.

Likewise, the relationship of friendship with Jesus is in the context of election (Jn. 15:16): 'You did not choose me, but I chose you, and appointed you to go out and bear fruit.' Sadly, this concept of election no longer warms our hearts with amazement at God's grace. The doctrine of election has become an arid theological debate between predestination and free will. But that is not the issue which Jesus is addressing. Election is something beautiful – 'I chose you', Jesus said. Surely those first disciples must have asked themselves why Jesus chose them? Jesus was the King of Kings, the Lord of Lords, with all glory at his fingertips. He had the power to choose whoever he wanted. He could have chosen the top rabbis, the best Sadducees or Pharisees; he could have chosen the millionaires or popular people. Indeed he could have chosen whoever he wanted, but he chose that little band of twelve men. I often like to picture their amazement. I imagine them looking in their mirrors (an anachronism!) and asking themselves why Jesus chose them. He could have chosen anybody. We today may follow in the footsteps of the disciples' amazement at Jesus' gracious choice of them. When we go to church on a Sunday we may look around at those seated near us, feeling, 'If I had been the Lord of glory, I would not have chosen them!' But the friendship of Jesus springs from the sure reality of his election, that he chose the twelve disciples and he has chosen us and the other Christians around us. The glorious reality of our election impels us to bow before the Lord in grateful adoration. And he has chosen us that we might bear fruit.

Then, too, in John 15 Jesus' choice of us as his friends is bracketed by the call to love one another – 'My command is this, love one another as I have loved you' (Jn. 15:12), and

'This is my command, love each other' (Jn. 15:17). This emphasis in John 15 fits the model of God's relationships within the Trinity – relationships of loving harmony and unity. The pattern for the church is to be one of love.

It is with this background of Jesus' words on relationships of love that Paul wrote his letter to the Philippians. He wanted to thank them for a gift, but he also wanted to exhort the Philippian church to love with one heart, one mind and one spirit. He exhorted them to be humble like Jesus in order that they could be united in harmony. He wrote to them in this way because there were two women in the church who were quarrelling. Such lack of love on the part of Syntyche and Euodia constituted a negation of the gospel of Christ. If there is no harmony in a church, the message is lost, because it fails to follow the pattern of loving relationships in the Trinity. Disunity negates the message of forgiveness, love and reconciliation. If there are two people in a church who do not love each other, this represents a major problem. As friends of Jesus we are to love one another.

Parables: Ears to hear?

Jesus shares with his friends everything that the Father has given him. 'I have called you friends, because everything I learnt from my Father I have made known to you' (Jn. 15:15). With his friends and followers he does not speak in parables, as he does with other people. But to his disciples he explains everything (Mk. 4:34), because it has been given to them to know the secrets of the kingdom of God. He therefore speaks clearly to them.

Jesus' parables have a dual purpose. Jesus tells parables in order that those who have ears may hear, and those who do not have ears to hear will not hear. His disciples should understand the meaning of his parabolic teaching, while his opponents' ears will be stopped so that they will not understand. So it is with the parabolic expression which Jesus uses of himself. Again and again he calls himself the Son of Man; and the disciples gradually come to know what that means. They related it to Daniel 7 and so to the divine calling of Jesus. They knew what it meant in the context of Daniel 7. But Ezekiel also uses the expression 'Son of Man'. Whereas in Daniel 'Son of Man' clearly contains divine significance, in Ezekiel it merely means a human being. The opponents of Jesus may oppose him for other reasons, but they do not attack him because of his use of the title 'Son of Man'. They failed to see the true meaning of Jesus' use of this title; and they could understand 'Son of Man' from its Ezekiel background. To the disciples, however, it was clear what Jesus meant. From the earliest explanations of 'Son of Man' in the New Testament and in church history we find that the church has never doubted the divine significance of Daniel 7 as the background to this title. Jesus makes it clear to his disciples, but not to those who radically opposed him. This is important for our mission today. Sometimes as Christians we are naïve and want to make the gospel clear to everybody. But the pattern of Jesus is to be absolutely clear in teaching those with ears, those who are followers or open to becoming followers of Jesus. To such people we want to make the gospel clear as we ought to speak (Col. 4:4) But with those who are violently opposed to the gospel we may be wise to be unclear. We may face situations where an unequivocal presentation of the gospel will only result in our being assaulted and the name of Christ being blasphemed. Following in the footsteps of Jesus, it might be right to speak parabolically so that they will not understand. But with the disciples Jesus taught with openness and clarity. We are not to cast our pearls before swine, otherwise they will turn on us and rend us asunder (Mt. 7:6). But with the disciples Jesus was open and clear.

Diversity

Jesus chooses as his friends and disciples people from a rich variety of backgrounds. Some were very gifted but unreliable, like Peter; some powerful but objectionable – 'sons of thunder'. Christians like Peter or James and John can cause considerable problems in a church or mission team, but Jesus took that risk. He not only dares to risk failure but, in fact, he even incurs failure. Judas betrays him and Peter denies him, despite his deep love. So Jesus' disciples include the gifted and unreliable, the powerful and objectionable. But also there are the quieter, more ordinary disciples, who appear to be non-entities. Indeed, in the list of the twelve disciples there are several of whom nothing further is heard. We hardly know who they were. They were not striking leaders; as far as we know they did not do great works afterwards; several of them seem to have been singularly ordinary people. Jesus' was not a monochrome team, it was a very richly diverse team.

At All Nations Christian College we have tried to follow this pattern in our choice of staff. We want every staff member to come from a different background with varying experience. Each should be quite different in personality and temperament, as also in spiritual and theological emphases within the broad spectrum of evangelical approaches. Each should have a unique contribution to share with the whole college family. A former principal used to say that the staff team should be like an orchestra where each member is playing a different instrument, but under the direction of the divine conductor a beautiful harmony should emerge.

Jesus' example in choosing such a diverse group of disciples is a model not only for a college, but equally for a church or missionary agency. In many ways it is less challenging when 'birds of a feather flock together', but a diverse team with varying gifts and emphases can have a wider ministry which relates to a wider spectrum of people. In a richly diverse team each member will have their particular gifts and will have much to learn to learn from one another.

We may think of Jesus' disciples as a group and refer to them corporately as 'the twelve'. In actual fact they were a group of individuals who needed to be moulded together into a harmonious team, in which they lovingly accepted and enjoyed their difference. The relationships between Jesus and his disciples stand as a model for the church of God. This model contradicts the modern emphasis on homogeneous units, in which separate churches should be formed only from one distinct culture, ethnic group or generation. In following the model of Jesus and his disciples, unity in diversity needs also to be underlined. The love of God breaks down the sinful barriers of the generation gap, different styles of music, of racial, cultural or class prejudice.

Shepherd and sheep

Jesus also relates to his disciples like a shepherd with his sheep. The Middle Eastern shepherd always walks in front of his sheep or goats, and the animals follow the shepherd. There is a relationship of dual responsibility. Jesus has a responsibility for his followers – he cares for them, looks after them, providing for them in love. And we as believers in Jesus are to follow him. Following always has a double significance. It has the significance of following him as

Lord, and therefore living in obedience to him. Obedience may not be a popular concept in modern society, but as Christians we are called to obey Jesus Christ as our Lord. His word has authority over us.

Secondly, to follow Jesus means that Christians are to pattern their lives on the life of Jesus. The believer's relationships should follow the model of Jesus' relationship to his disciples. Matthew's gospel particularly emphasizes that Jesus is the *didáskalos* (teacher). As such, he is the second Moses who gives us a new law. Commentators differ as to whether the five didactic sections in Matthew's Gospel are intended to parallel the five books of Moses in the Pentateuch, but clearly Jesus taught his followers a superior way of righteousness which bore the stamp of his own authority – 'You have heard that it was said . . . but I say to you . . .' (Mt. 5:21, 27, 31, 33, 38, 43).

The Greek word *mathētēs* (disciple) conveys the other side of the coin. A teacher requires those who will sit at his feet to learn. Following Jesus as his disciple requires the humility to become a learner, submitting our thinking and worldview to him as teacher.

Neither the precepts and commands of the Mosaic law nor the new covenant of Jesus is merely a list of taboos. They are based on the character of God himself in order to help God's people to be holy as he is holy, modelling their lives on the life of Jesus. This may be more clearly understood by contrasting biblical law with the Shari'ah, the law of Islam. In Islam, law is a set of commandments which have no basis in the character of God. They are taboo laws, consisting of arbitrary do's and don'ts which are not based on the character or nature of God himself. This means that a prophet like Mohammed can be above the law because those taboos do not bind a prophet. Thus other people may only have four wives, but the prophet can have twelve. Likewise, when believers reach paradise they may have a multitude of brown-eyed maidens to serve them with golden goblets of wine. On earth the taboo of law forbids alcohol, but in heaven alcoholic drink in profusion is permitted. Such a concept of freedom is unthinkable in the Christian concept of law. As followers of Jesus we are called to obey his commands because they are based on the character of God. Therefore a saintly person or a prophet is to be even more holy than other people. And in heaven the people of God will be perfectly holy, absolutely like him. Eternal life in heaven is not for the Christian an antinomian freedom, but rather the perfection of a life perfectly moulded into the character of God himself.

The missionary task is therefore not just to make converts, not just to call people to salvation. In the great commission in Matthew 28 Christ's followers were called to make disciples of all nations. The work of mission is not only evangelism and church planting; it is not complete until people become disciples of Jesus in obedience to his word and in humbly learning from him.

In some cultures it is difficult to bring people into a relationship with Jesus; but when they do come into a relationship with him, it is relatively easy to bring them into the maturity of discipleship. In some other cultures and situations the reverse is true. It is easy to bring people into a profession of faith in Jesus, but much more difficult for them to grow into mature disciples. To be specific, in western Europe it is difficult to bring people to commit themselves to Jesus Christ, but when they do make a profession of commitment to him, then it is relatively easy to disciple them. On the contrary, in many black African cultures, as also in the Philippines and in some South American contexts, it is easy to call people to conversion, and people often respond spontaneously. But to help them to become settled disciples of Jesus is much more difficult. In the modern mission movement in Britain some Christians go overseas on mission trips for a fortnight's preaching or visiting missionaries. They often come back with exciting stories, particularly from black Africa. They recount how they preached and hundreds of people responded to the evangelistic appeal. The question remains: did they become disciples? Because that is the heart of the Christian faith and of mission – to become learners of Jesus, not just converts.

All the biblical metaphors of relationship, such as those of shepherd and follower, teacher and learner, must be regarded in the context of a personal relationship with Jesus. So Jesus says, 'This is eternal life, that they may know you, the only true God, and Jesus Christ whom you have sent' (Jn. 17:3). The key to relationships and to eternal life is therefore the personal knowledge of God the Father and Jesus Christ whom the Father has sent. When Jesus calls his disciples to himself and says to them, 'Follow me', he immediately instructs them to be with him (Mk. 3:14). His call is threefold – the disciples are called to be with him, to be sent out to preach, and then also to have authority even to cast out demons. But 'to be with him' is primary. The words indicate that intimacy of relationship which lies at the very heart of our faith.

As we communicate the gospel to those of other faiths, this reality of an intimate relationship with the Lord will naturally appeal to some people, including mystics of all faiths – particularly Sufi Muslims and Kabbalistic Jews. It will also prove attractive to Bhakti Hindus. On the other hand, it will seem radically new to most orthodox Muslims, as also to most orthodox Jews. It may appear almost incomprehensible to most Buddhists or Hindus, or Confucianists. Whether the call to an intimate relationship with God is attractive to people or not, it must always remain central to the gospel message. The command of Jesus is not just to believe in him, nor just to obey or serve him, but it is indeed to love him. The greatest commandment is, 'Thou shalt love the Lord thy God with all thy heart' (Mt. 22:37).

Moving towards one another: One step at a time

In the New Testament account of Jesus' relationships with his followers there is a consistent idea of motion towards. Relationships are not static. Thus, in Matthew's Gospel, verbs of motion are emphasized. Matthew uses verbs which show movement towards Jesus, and Jesus moving towards people. We observe this emphasis in the frequent use of verbs with the prefix *pros* (towards). The preposition *pros* is often translated in English as 'with', for example in John 1 where the Word was *pros theon* (Jn. 1:1). This is commonly translated as 'with God', and some commentaries strongly maintain that *pros* does not signify motion. They stress that the Word was 'with God' and in no way moving towards God. Nevertheless, we should note that in all relationships there is a continuous moving towards the other. So Jesus is not only with the Father, but also constantly going towards him. Likewise our relationship with God in Christ involves a purposeful moving towards God. This is equally true of marriage or other human relationships. Wonderfully in his grace and love God also moves towards us and comes to us. So we are called to move consciously towards, as well as being with, God and our neighbour. This process of moving towards one another is not just physical, but also spiritual, mental and emotional. It involves our whole personality.

Jesus not only moves towards us but he is also very gracious in leading his disciples on one step at a time. He does not suddenly parachute his disciples into what is unacceptable to them, but he gradually moves them forward he leads us one step at a time. Later in this book we shall see this truth as Jesus challenges his disciples to develop their mission outreach from just their own Jewish people to the Samaritans and then to the Gentiles.

Jesus also develops his people in their understanding of who he is. This is particularly important in mission among Muslims, but it relates also to all forms of mission. In our evangelistic work we need to remember how Jesus developed the understanding and faith of his disciples until they finally grasped who he really was. Initially they met a man walking by the Sea of Galilee. We know in hindsight that this man was God incarnate, but they did not yet know that. The Jesus whom they met was very obviously a man. He was walking in a natural human way by the Sea of Galilee, but there must have been something quite magnetic about his whole personality. So when he said 'Follow me', they immediately got up from their fishing nets or their tax tables, left everything and followed him. In the following months they stayed with him, lived with him, watched him and related to him. As they observed his miracles, heard his teaching and saw his relationships both with other people and themselves, they began to see that this was not just an ordinary man walking by the Sea of Galilee. He was a distinctly special man.

Each of the Gospels describes the major turning point of Caesarea Philippi, where Peter led the disciples in the new confession of faith: 'You are the Messiah, the son of the living God' (Mt. 16:16). Jewish theology does not attribute divinity to the Messiah, so when Peter calls Jesus the Messiah, he probably did not mean that Jesus was God incarnate. He presumably meant that Jesus was the long-awaited deliverer, the liberating saviour, the one who would come to save his people. Peter was acknowledging Jesus to be the Messiah, the anointed King, the son of the living God. Traditional Christian theology has normally assumed that the titles 'Son of God' and 'Messiah' in Peter's confession attribute divinity to Jesus. But in a Jewish context it is more likely that 'Son of God' is a title of perfect humanity, of absolute God-like perfection. Thus in the genealogy of Jesus Adam is also called the son of God (Lk. 3:38). If the title 'Son of God' implies divinity, we find ourselves with a theology not of a Trinity, but of a quadrennity – the Father, two sons (Jesus and Adam) and the Holy Spirit. But Israel, too, was called to be the children of God, to be like God in holiness and perfection, bringing glory and honour to God. This was how the Jews understood the title 'Son of God'. Nevertheless it should be emphasized that the Bible clearly affirms the divinity of Christ, but not because of the title 'Son of God'. There are many other proofs of the divinity of Jesus Christ. So the disciples, led by Peter, were beginning to see that Jesus was more than an ordinary man. He was the liberator, the long-awaited saviour, the king of the kingdom, absolutely perfect humanity in the image of God, holy as God is holy. Immediately after Peter's confession at Caesarea Philippi Jesus began to explain to the disciples that he must suffer and die (Mt. 16:21). They obviously did not understand him and again Peter leads them in objecting to the idea of Jesus suffering. Even when Jesus comes towards the end of his incarnate life and goes to his death on the cross, the disciples are evidently bewildered. They did not understand that Jesus was fulfilling what he had told them would happen. So the death of Jesus leaves them bewildered and confused – until the resurrection.

Then the disciples move on into a new stage of understanding of Jesus. Thomas now takes the lead with his marvelling exclamation, 'My Lord and my God!' (Jn. 20:28) And then comes Pentecost and the experience of the Holy Spirit, the third person of the Trinity. The disciples came from a strictly monotheistic background. Their whole faith rested on the foundational truth that the God of Israel is the only true God (see the creed of Israel in Dt. 6:4). But now the disciples had come to acknowledge Jesus as Lord and God – were there therefore two gods? And the experience of the person of the Holy Spirit only added to this theological conundrum – how can the one God coexist with Jesus Christ and the Holy Spirit also as God? The early centuries of Christian history witnessed the struggles of the church's attempts to understand and express theologically the glorious mystery of one God in Trinity. The example of Jesus leading his disciples on, one step at a time, is very relevant for Christian witness among Muslims, as also with Jews. As strong monotheists like the first disciples, they may begin their pilgrimage of faith by coming to admire the human Jesus. The more they learn about the life of Jesus, the more they will love him. At this stage the Christians' witness should avoid all debate and controversy concerning the deity of Jesus, his title 'Son of God' and the Trinity. Following on from their love for the man Jesus, they will hopefully grow to appreciate that Jesus is perfectly sinless, holy as God alone is holy. And they may accept the biblical teaching that Jesus has come as the saviour of the world to deliver his people from their sins and from all demonic oppression. At that stage, it becomes easier to talk about the controversial issues of the cross and the resurrection, the Holy Spirit and the Trinity.

I remember talking some years ago with a Sufi Muslim in Kabul, Afghanistan. He loved the human Jesus, so when he discovered that I believed in and followed Jesus, he smiled with delight. 'We are brothers', he said. 'Yes, Jesus is wonderful – when we know Jesus, we know God. When we see Jesus, we see God. Jesus is the way to God.' He had come to love and admire Jesus. But he still had not come to accept the death of Jesus on the cross, the deity of Jesus or the Holy Spirit. The Hindu Keshab Chandra Sen came to a very similar position. Of him it has been said, 'Christ became the centre of his life and the guiding force in all his thinking' (R. Boyd, *An Introduction to Indian Christian Theology*,

Madras: CLS, 1969). This was a man who loved Jesus, but he never became a Christian. He firmly rejected the Christian doctrine of the Trinity. But a man or woman who loves Jesus like K.C. Sen did may more easily accept the full biblical teaching concerning the cross and the resurrection, the deity of Christ and the Trinity. This gradual step-by-step leading into all truth is the pattern which Jesus has given us in his relationships with his disciples.

Passing on his ministry

Jesus is also very gracious with his disciples in training them by using them. He gives them a sense of worth, dignity and purpose by giving them work to do for him. This may be observed in the story of Jesus feeding the crowds, both the Jewish crowd of the 5,000 and the Gentile crowd of the 4,000. In both cases Jesus gives the food to the disciples and they give it to the people. When the disciples come to Jesus and say, 'This is a remote place, and it's already getting late. Send the crowds away so they can go to the villages and buy themselves some food' (Mt. 14:15), Jesus replies with simple but shocking clarity, 'They do not need to go away. You give them something to eat.' They faced a huge crowd of 5,000 men plus many women and children. When my wife and I worked in Indonesia we used to reckon that a typical family was a husband, a wife and six children. On this reckoning the crowd of 5,000 men may have totalled 40,000 people. 'You give them something to eat', Jesus calmly told them – imagine the shock and the horror. And they could only muster five loaves and two small fish. But Jesus has a purpose. When the crowd had been fed, the disciples must have felt a tremendous sense of elation. With Jesus they could have a ministry, they could do something of significance with him. It is always true that the Lord can do the task of mission much better without us, because we are apt to make a mess of everything we do in the church and in mission. But he graciously uses us in order to give us a sense of purpose and worth. We too are able to 'do something of significance with him'.

When our daughter was young, my wife took her into the kitchen one day and began to teach her cooking. When lunch was served, my daughter rather proudly said, 'Daddy, I cooked the lunch.' This was somewhat of an exaggeration! She had merely made the gravy or the custard – and it would probably have been less lumpy if Elizabeth had prepared it without her assistance. But children need to be patiently trained and taught. In this way they gain a sense of purpose and self-worth. Jesus graciously trains his disciples also.

My daughter's childlike pride, 'I cooked the lunch', is often mirrored in adult Christian workers – 'I preached', 'I taught', 'I am the servant of the Lord', 'I am the vicar'. The very words 'the Lord's servant' or 'the vicar/minister' are often spelled with a capital letter. One minister, in moving to a new church, complained, 'One problem here is that people in this church don't seem to have a proper sense of the dignity of the ministry.' In the New Testament the ministry goes together with being a slave of Christ and of fellow Christians. There is not much dignity in being a slave. Pride is natural to us all.

Jesus is realistic with his disciples. He knows their weaknesses. In Matthew, therefore, the disciples are known as 'the little ones', and Jesus calls them 'those of little faith', the *oligopistoi* or 'little faith people'. Although Jesus is realistic in recognizing the weakness of their faith, he still expects them to grow. And he leads them on with that purpose in mind. This may be seen in the two accounts in Matthew of Jesus walking on the water. In the first account when the disciples saw Jesus walking on the water and heard him rebuking the winds and the waves, they were amazed. They asked, 'What kind of man is this? Even the winds and the waves obey him' (Mt. 8:27). When they again saw Jesus walking on the lake and stilling the wind, they were initially terrified. But then they came to worship him, exclaiming, 'Surely this is the Son of God!' (Mt. 14:33). So the disciples moved on in their faith from 'What sort of man is this?' to a more confident 'You are the Son of God' and they worshipped him. They grew in their faith.

In his relationship with his disciples, Jesus shows great patience in forgiving and restoring them when they fall. So it was with Peter when he denied the Lord. Indeed Jesus does not merely restore them, but he shows his continued trust by giving them a ministry. To Peter, therefore, he entrusts the commission to 'Feed my sheep.'

Jesus passes his ministry on to his disciples, and then on through his disciples to us. Thus there is a continuity in the New Testament – the history and role of Israel climaxes in John the Baptist, the greatest prophet of the Old Testament era. Then John the Baptist gives way to Jesus, so the preached message of John the Baptist becomes the basis for Jesus' message – 'Repent, for the kingdom of heaven is at hand' (Mt. 3:2; 4:17). And when John the Baptist is killed, then Jesus knows that he is going to be killed (Mt. 14). There is a definite continuity – Israel, John the Baptist, Jesus, and on from Jesus to his disciples. So Jesus commissions his disciples, 'As the Father has sent me, even so I send you' (Jn. 20:21). This continuity and development of ministry thus passes from Jesus through the history of the church to us.

This biblical continuity disallows such glib Christian statements as: 'Pentecost is the birthday of the Christian church.' The Christian church is a continuity, developing out from the Old Testament people of God and the congregation of Israel. The Greek word for church, *ekklēsía* is the translation of *qahal* or *edah*, the Hebrew words for the congregation of Israel. Likewise in Romans 11, Paul writes of the tree of Israel which has some of the branches pruned away. Then the Gentile branches are grafted in, but the old tree is not cut down or a new tree planted. The same old tree with its roots deeply planted in the ancient history of Israel now has a wide variety of branches. Jewish, Samaritan and Gentile branches of every tribe, tongue, people and nation belong together in the *qahal* of God's people.

As Jesus passes on the baton of his ministry to his people, he also empowers them by the gift of the Holy Spirit. Jesus himself was empowered by the Spirit. Although accused of casting out demons by the power of Beelzebub, Jesus truly did so by the Spirit (Mt. 12:24–28). So when Jesus passes on his ministry to his disciples, he not only sends them out but also breathes the Holy Spirit upon them (Jn. 20:21). It is noteworthy that this is paralleled in Acts 1:8 where Jesus' command to be a witness to all nations goes hand in hand with the empowering of the Holy Spirit. The church of God needs the power of the Holy Spirit for the task of mission together with his authority and presence.

We conclude this chapter with one final point concerning Jesus' relationship with his followers. He shares a life of suffering with his disciples, so that Christians can find *koinonia* with Christ in his sufferings (Phil. 3:10). Jesus gives his disciples a model of suffering, having nowhere to lay his head (Mt. 8:20). He is the suffering God of whom K. Kitamori writes in his *A Theology of the Pain of God*. Kitamori sees Jeremiah 31:20 as the kernel of the biblical faith on the nature of God in action which he summarizes in the formula $L + W = P$ (love plus wrath equals pain). The combination of deep love and holy anger produces an agony of suffering in the very heart of God. The God revealed to us in Scripture is not a God of prosperity only, but of suffering as well. And Jesus as God incarnate also suffers.

Jesus prepares his disciples to walk in his suffering foot-steps not only by setting them an example, but also by showing them more clearly who he is and what he can provide. So when he becomes agonizingly aware of his impending death through the beheading of his predecessor (Mt. 14:1–13), knowing therefore that his disciples will also have to follow him in suffering, he reveals his messianic calling by feeding the Jewish 5,000 and the Gentile 4,000. Between these two events he walks on the water and stills the storm. He then performs a healing miracle for a Gentile woman, an act which introduces the feeding of the Gentile crowd. With this chain of significant events Jesus builds up the disciples' confidence in him as Messiah and prepares them to fulfil their calling to suffer with and for him.

My wife and I once visited in northwest China and went to the city where her parents used to be missionaries. One of the leaders of the church there said to us, 'The missionaries of the China Inland Mission set us an example of suffering and we have walked in their footsteps.' Jesus set a model of suffering in his ministry, and that is the model in which the disciples walked. We in mission today are to set a model of suffering for the gospel, whatever it costs, that we might pass on that heritage to others.

3

Jesus' Relationships with his Opponents

Many of us find it not too difficult to form relationships with friends, but how do we relate to those who oppose us? We can learn much from the way Jesus handled his enemies. He always treated them with dignity and yet never allowed them to manipulate him. Throughout the history of the church and mission God's people have continually had to relate to people who reject Christ and resist his followers.

Compassion for the crowds

But before we consider those who strongly opposed Jesus we notice another group of people. Caught in the middle ground between the increasingly antagonistic Scribes and Pharisees on the one hand, and Jesus with his disciples on the other, are found the crowds, the *ochlos*. Translations may vary in seeing them as 'the crowds', 'the people', or 'the multitude'; but the *ochlos* is that uncertain and unreliable majority of people who move easily from love to hatred, or vice versa, according to circumstances. Those designated by this term consisted of the large majority of ordinary people – peasant farmers and fishermen, women and children, the poor and the marginalized. Most of them will not have attended a rabbinic school and so were considered 'ignorant' and 'untaught' by the more educated. They were powerless, having no political or economic influence. They were oppressed by the Romans wielding their ruthless imperial power, and they were despised by the leaders of the people of Israel. This large group surrounding Jesus constantly swung back and forth in uncertain allegiance. What attitude did Jesus show to them?

From early on in Jesus' ministry we notice the crowds beginning to gather. Sometimes they obstruct his desire for solitude and for prayer, and Jesus tries to escape them. His action may be a model for Christian missionaries facing the pressure of constant crowds, particularly in overpopulated cities and in cultures where privacy is not valued. Those who come from rather private cultures in the west may find crowds quite oppressive. They may need to follow Jesus' example in consciously seeking solitude and quiet prayer on their own. From time to time they may need to escape.

Sometimes the crowds are moved to follow Jesus. We have already observed, particularly in Matthew's gospel, the double significance of following Jesus as Lord and as example. As missionaries in the Karo Batak churches of North Sumatra, Indonesia, we were struck by the fact that at that time the Christians there used a different vocabulary (not just a different language, but different vocabulary within that language) from us in the west. We often emphasize new birth and being born again as the Shibboleth to show that we are truly alive in our faith and genuine in loving the Lord. The Karo Batak Christians, however, commonly asked the question, 'Do you follow Jesus?' For them this was the Shibboleth – are people truly following Jesus? They contrasted that to being merely a 'skin Christian' – one who looks outwardly Christian and performs the right Christian activities, but when scratched

Rows
EWISH/GENTILE

is quite pagan underneath in their heart. The opposite of a 'skin Christian' was someone who truly modelled their life on Jesus and followed him as Lord. So the key question was, 'Do you follow Jesus?' The original call to the twelve disciples was not to be born again but to follow Jesus.

When Jesus looked on the multitudes he had compassion on them (Mt. 9:36). Jesus' 'looking' was not just a casual glance, for the use of the Greek word signifies a careful observation. He looked at the crowds, he saw them, and then as a result he had compassion on them. The same thought occurs again in Matthew's Gospel when Jesus saw the Jewish crowd of 5,000 and then the Gentile crowd of 4,000. With the Gentile crowd Jesus took the initiative with his disciples and said, 'I have compassion on the crowd' (Mt. 15:32). His words imply a rebuke of his disciples – they evidently showed inadequate compassion towards the Gentile crowd. Were they racially prejudiced? When faced with a Jewish crowd, the disciples took the initiative in informing Jesus of the crowd's need and suggesting a remedy (Mt. 14:15). Jesus looked both on the Jewish and the Gentile crowds with compassion.

Jesus' compassion presents us with a model which relates both to mission overseas and to mission in our own country. When we commute to work on a crowded train or in rush-hour traffic, what reaction do we have? Do we look at the crowds and see them as sheep without a shepherd? Or in the selfishness of a frenetic life do we edge them aside and wish we could be rid of them? Jesus sets a model of looking perceptively at the crowds and having compassion on them. As we jostle with the crowds in the supermarket or on busy streets, it is Christ-like to look into people's eyes and see their individual significance. When western missionaries first go overseas and find themselves in the midst of the crowds of a two-thirds world city, the concept of having compassion on the crowds becomes vitally important.

Western Christians are particularly interested in individuals, but relate with more difficulty to crowds. Jesus *was* of course interested in individuals and related to them, but he also related to the crowds and had compassion on them.

When my wife and I first went to Singapore in 1960, it was a much smaller city than it is now. Nevertheless, by British standards it was a large and busy city. I remember standing one day in one of the new housing areas with huge blocks of flats stretching into the sky above me. One block stood next to another, and the crowds flowed past me in their thousands. The experience of standing alone in the midst of the throng with the high blocks of flats dwarfing me made me feel my insignificance. But it also challenged me to look on the crowds and have compassion. Jesus' compassion moved him so strongly that he wept over Jerusalem, knowing the tragedy of judgement that was to be their sad future. He was moved as he saw the tragedy of that city which God specially loved and for whose peace all Jews pray. The compassion of God stands out as a preeminent characteristic of his nature.

The biblical description of God is not of a cool, unemotional being sitting on the top of Mount Olympus. He does not look down from on high at the multitudes as if they were little ants running hither and thither. God is deeply involved in the history of the world, actively demonstrating his compassion. God's warm, heart-felt empathy with human beings may be contrasted with the reactions of Allah in Islam. In one of the Hadith Qudsi, a holy tradition supposedly containing a verbatim quotation from God himself, God says, 'These to heaven and I care not, these to hell, and I care not.' Allah is too great to be emotionally involved in this world or to feel human emotions. He feels no pleasure at people going into paradise. He does not share in the joy of their salvation. Nor, on the other hand, is Allah moved with compassion and sadness at the tragic horror of judgement. But Jesus is not like the Muslim Allah; he rejoices in his followers' faith and righteousness. Likewise he is moved with compassion. He sees the crowds and weeps over Jerusalem.

Jesus' compassion leads to an active ministry, seeking the welfare and salvation of the crowds. He feeds the crowds, he heals their sick and casts out their demons, and he teaches and instructs them. His arms are outstretched to welcome the multitudes, including the poor and the despised.

Although Jesus has compassion on the crowds, and in his ministry seeks to win them to become his followers, he does not pander to their hunger for the sensational. He does not provide miraculous signs just to satisfy their desire for exciting and tangible proofs that he is the Messiah. Nor does he give in to their wish that he should be a political king, a deliverer from Roman imperialism. He makes no compromise in order to gain popularity or support, but he steadily pursues his path according to the Father's will. Christian preachers and speakers know the temptation to mould their message to fit the taste of their audience in order to gain popularity and esteem. There is only a thin dividing line between such compromise and a right desire to be relevant. Jesus *does* relate to the needs and thinking of his hearers. His message and his life are identified with them, but he does not compromise in order to gain popular favour. As a result, the crowds are disillusioned and disappointed in Jesus. They forsake him and cease to follow him. Thus the fickle crowds welcome Jesus to Jerusalem with cries of 'Hosanna/Save us' and lay a carpet of palm fronds on the street before him. But they quickly become disillusioned and betray him with the call of the mob: 'Crucify him!'

In every part of the world crowds are fickle and popular opinion is not to be trusted. Crowds tend to waver – one moment being positive and negative the next. Church and mission history exemplify this sad reality. In mission history we observe again and again how the church is developed in a particular area or amongst a particular people. Often a difficult and unresponsive start leads into something of a mass movement. The crowds turn to the Lord and the times of faithful sowing seem to have produced an abundant harvest. Then a new anti-Christian leader gains power, or something happens that causes disillusionment. Suddenly the young church faces a period of persecution. This pattern may be seen in the history of the church in Madagascar. A mass movement to Christ was followed by persecution of the most ferocious nature. Only after this persecution did the remnants of the church form the foundation of a more stable ongoing movement of God. Similar stories can be found again and again in the history of the church. The history of the Reformation in Europe gives us a further example of this pattern. Whole peoples turned to the new, reformed faith, in mass movements led by their political leaders. Then a new prince came to power or the authorities came under the influence of the Jesuit counter-reformation. Suddenly the whole of Austria or some other state would turn back into the old form of unreformed Catholicism, and the cries of the crowds changed their tune.

Ultimately, however, as we look at the crowds, we have to say that in the Gospels there are no neutrals. Although the crowds seem to be somewhere between being followers of Jesus and being opponents of Jesus, ultimately there is nothing in between. Jesus says that we are either for him or against him. He says it both ways – if we are not for him, we are against him, but likewise, if we are not against him, we are for him. John's Gospel underlines this reality with its stark contrasts between believing and not believing, light and darkness, love and hatred, eternal life and the abiding wrath of God. Finally even the crowds have to come off the fence and take sides either for or against Jesus.

The suffering God

In the midst of the crowds there are also the marginalized – the sick, orphans, widows and other women, as well as such social outcasts as the tax collectors. In the Gospels Jesus is shown to take particular concern for the poor and the powerless. He scandalized the respectable leaders of society by associating with outcast publicans and sinners. He befriended a prostitute, touched the untouchable leprosy sufferers, healed Gentiles and women, raised to life a poor widow's only son and restored the demon-possessed to health.

As I look at the British church today, it seems to me that we are facing something of a paradox. The growing influence of prosperity theology is clearly observable in the lives even of many churches which in theory strongly reject such teaching. There is a tendency to feel that a Spirit-filled Christian leader ought to have a smart, fast car, a large house and eat in expensive restaurants. This prosperity lifestyle, even if not technically a prosperity theology, coexists with a deep concern for, and emphasis on preaching to, the marginalized. Worship songs of this character repeatedly stress victory, winning and power, with the pulling down of enemy strongholds, rather than emphasizing suffering with Christ. Yet at the same time those influenced by prosperity theology may display a biblical emphasis on Jesus' particular concern for the poor, the despised and the marginalized. It is not easy, either in teaching or in practice, to hold together in creative tension the paradox of God's power, victory and lavish generosity to his people as well as his suffering and identification with the poor.

The nature of God as revealed in Christ and in the Scriptures is not only one of victorious power. But God also is a suffering God. Therefore he has tremendous empathy

with those who suffer. Jesus is the suffering servant, not the
victorious servant only. In various more recent western
theological books, for example Fretheim, as also in earlier
Japanese theology, there has been an emphasis on a God
who suffers (T.E. Fretheim, *The Suffering of God: An Old
Testament Perspective* [Philadelphia: Fortress Press,
1984]). This insight into the nature of God revealed in
Scripture evokes a consistently warm response among
Japanese Bible students, as it has been my privilege to
experience in tutoring such students at All Nations
Christian College. In Japanese literature through the
centuries the hero has often been one who suffers. The more
modern history of the Second World War has further
contributed to the sense that as Japanese they are a suffering
people.

As we have seen in the formula of K. Kitamori, $L + W = P$,
God is a God who in himself combines love and holy anger.
Love on its own without holy anger has no pain. Grandpar-
ents may appreciate this truth. They can enjoy the fun of
grandchildren's naughtiness without the responsibility of
holy discipline. Love without holy anger has no pain. It is so
much easier to be a grandparent than to be a parent. But the
biblical God is our father, not just a grandfather. His love
includes perfect holiness which cannot tolerate evil.

Likewise, wrath without love has no pain. It is easy to
watch television or read the newspapers, observing with
critical superiority the terrible things that other people are
doing – cruel genocide, savage rapes and murders, fearful
deeds and systems of injustice. We may be provoked into
real anger but we do not know or love the people concerned. Because the anger may lack personal involvement
or any relationship of love, it can often be laid aside under
the pressures of our own daily lives. Without true love,
self-centredness inevitably prevails. So wrath without love
involves no pain. But God is not like that. In Jeremiah 31:20

God calls Ephraim 'my dear son'. Ephraim is the child in whom he delights. The words of God in this verse resonate with deep love. And yet God has to speak in judgement against Ephraim. The combination of holy judgement and wrath together with a heartfelt love is striking. But God remembers Ephraim and is associated with him. He not only 'remembers' Ephraim and has 'great compassion' for him, but God also declares, 'therefore my heart yearns for him'. The German translation of this Hebrew word *hamah* in the Luther translation is *'darum bricht mir mein Herz'* – my heart breaks within me. *Hamah* is a word of suffering, a word of pain. It is used when a large wave breaks and the water crashes all over the place. It is used of a bird or chicken that is frightened and begins to flutter in chaotic distress and disturbance. It is used of a mighty wind which sweeps all before it in uncontrolled destruction. Perhaps the King James Version has the most apposite translation. Delightfully, it puts into the mouth of God the antiquated words: 'My bowels are pained'. Those of us who have suffered 'Delhi belly' will identify with the extreme pain of this expression. God says that his heart is pained because of the sin of Israel. God suffers as his love joins hands with his absolute holiness.

God also suffers with the marginalized. Just as God is one who suffers, so also his son Jesus Christ reveals that he walks in his Father's suffering footsteps in his own life and ministry. This is evident right from the start of the ministry of Jesus. So his life starts with the slaughter of the innocents and his own exile to Egypt. His adult ministry also commences with his temptation in the wilderness. Here he endured forty days of deprivation and, in his weakness, the onslaughts of Satan. His own suffering gave him an empathy with the bruised and wounded of this world. This became the hallmark of his ministry.

Jesus emphasizes this already in the Nazareth declaration in the synagogue in Luke 4. At the outset of his life's work he announces his 'Jubilee year programme' for the sake of the poor, the captive, the blind and the oppressed. The essential purpose of God in Christ can be seen in this manifesto. Jesus' ministry is concerned with good news for the poor, with proclaiming freedom for the prisoners, recovery of sight for the blind, releasing the oppressed, and in his Jubilee declaration he proclaims the year of the Lord's favour. This is the text, therefore, on which the sermon of Jesus' life and ministry develops. Although Jesus never discriminates against the wealthy or powerful if they come humbly to him, he has a particular penchant for the poor.

Kraybill talks in his book of 'the upside down kingdom' (D.B. Kraybill, *The Upside-Down Kingdom* [London: Marshall, Morgan & Scott, 1985]). As we have seen, the Gospels show Jesus relating very specially to the poor, to prostitutes like Mary Magdalene, to women caught in adultery, to outcasts, leprosy sufferers, to the demon possessed, to women and children, to tax collectors, to the traitors and collaborators of that period. In chapter 4 we shall see how Jesus relates not only to his own Jewish people, but also to the Samaritans and the Gentiles – those who the Jews looked down on as inferior people who were outside God's covenant.

These verses in Luke 4 not only stress Jesus' concern for the poor, but they also underline the significance of preaching and proclaiming the gospel: 'The Spirit of the Lord is on me, because he has anointed me to *preach* good news to the poor. He has sent me to *proclaim* freedom for the prisoners and recovery of sight for the blind, to release the oppressed, to *proclaim* the year of the Lord's favour.' Through this three-fold repetition of 'preach' and 'proclaim', a social ministry to the poor and the oppressed is inseparably linked to a ministry of verbal proclamation. In the ministry of

Jesus, and therefore also in that of his church, the preached word and active care for the needy cannot be separated.

In Matthew's Gospel the ministry of the kingdom starts with suffering. Thus in Matthew 4:12 Jesus hears of the suffering of John the Baptist and this triggers his announcement of the kingdom: 'When Jesus heard that John had been put in prison, he returned to Galilee . . . From that time on Jesus began to preach, "Repent, for the kingdom of heaven is near." ' When Jesus heard about the suffering of the man of God, then he knew that the kingdom was near. In the Old Testament and in traditional Jewish teaching one of the conditions of the kingdom is always that suffering comes first. Suffering introduces and precedes the coming of the kingdom. There can be no resurrection without death first. There can be no new life without mortification of one's self. There can be no new tree without the seed first dying. The fearful battles with Gog and Magog besieging God's people (Rev. 20:7–11) will, however, give way to the sovereign reign of the Lord on his 'great white throne'.

Jesus' call to 'Repent, for the kingdom of heaven is near', leads immediately to his choice of the first four of his disciples, Peter and Andrew, James and John (Mt. 4:17–22). The vital element in Jesus' call of these disciples is that they are to 'follow' him and so to begin a close relationship with him. As a consequence of following Jesus they will be given the ministry of becoming fishers of men and women. But what does it mean to follow Jesus, the king of the kingdom? Jesus proceeds as the great teacher to expound a message which reveals God's character and purposes in his kingdom. Jesus is the second Moses, bringing God's new word. So his announcing the kingdom in Matthew 4 and his choice of the first disciples for the kingdom leads into the Sermon on the Mount (Mt. 5–7), in which Jesus teaches about the life and values of the kingdom. We must not separate Matthew 5–7 and the *preached* word from

Matthew 8 and the *acted* word. In Matthew 8 Jesus heals a
leprosy sufferer (vv. 1–4) and then in verses 5–13 he does a
miracle for a Gentile, a Roman centurion. He follows this
with a healing miracle for Peter's mother-in-law. In the
chauvinistic society of that time not only leprosy sufferers
and Gentiles, but also women, were treated as a powerless
underclass – and surely mothers-in-law qualify as a
despised category of people! In the acted word of Matthew
8, therefore, Jesus is working on behalf of the needy, the
despised and the oppressed. The kingdom has indeed
arrived. This is the context of chapter 8:18–22 where Jesus
solemnly declares that foxes have holes and birds of the air
have nests, but the Son of Man has no place to lay his head.
Following Jesus in the kingdom will be a sacrificial calling.
'Follow me and let the dead bury their own dead', he
exhorted them. The suffering of the kingdom touches even
the most sacred family responsibilities.

These words are followed by a passage that we shall
examine in the next chapter – Jesus stilling the storm on his
way to the Gentile land of Gadara (Mt. 8:23–27), as he
moves out of Israel into the region of the Gadarenes – into
the Gentile world.

Jesus and his opponents

Jesus relates not only to the ambivalent crowds and the
marginalized in their weakness and poverty, but also to
those who strongly opposed him. Even from his birth Jesus
is faced with fierce and ruthless opposition. Right at the
beginning of Jesus' life the Herod of that time caused
tremendous danger in his murderous determination to wipe
out any possible threat to his power as king. Jesus as
messianic king seemed potentially to be a dangerous rival.
Matthew stresses that Jesus was indeed born king of the

Jews – the accusation that was later to be publicly declared in what was written above his cross. The claim that Jesus was king only intensified Herod's insecure fear in his position as king – opposition often comes from insecurity and fear. In all situations where Christians are vehemently opposed or attacked, it is well to remember the background of such attacks in insecurity and fear. Right from the start of the Gospels' accounts of Jesus' life it is noticeable how his opponents demonstrate a definite dishonesty. Herod lies about wanting to worship the king, and seeks therefore to deceive the wise men. This leads to the ferocious miscarriage of justice in the murder of the infants. This is paralleled in the account of the end of Jesus' life. Again dishonesty rears its ugly head. The leaders of Israel at that time show no concern for truth, but they manipulate the crowds and pervert the judicial system. The authorities plot together to connive in a gross miscarriage of justice in the trial of Jesus. Blatant untruths prevail in the final story of Jesus' condemnation. And at the resurrection the leaders of Israel bribe the soldiers guarding the tomb to spread lies. Thus all the various movements in Israel's leadership – the Pharisees, Sadducees and scribes – join hands with the crowds and the Gentiles in dishonest opposition to Jesus. As the life of Jesus unfolds in the Gospels, the opposition to Jesus gradually increases. At first the Jewish leaders are relatively mild in their dislike of Jesus, but as the story develops the opposition increases in intensity. But we see too that Jesus responds increasingly vehemently. This could almost be seen as a growing reaction to their opposition. Paradoxically, in his trial and crucifixion Jesus no longer opposes his opponents. He no longer rebukes them strongly but rather submits ultimately like a sheep ready to be slaughtered. He does not open his mouth to defend himself or to attack his accusers; and finally he prays, 'Father, forgive them, because they really don't know what they're doing.'

This attitude of Jesus raises big issues concerning our reactions as Christians when we come under unwarranted and malicious attack. For example, this matter was seriously discussed in a Missionary Society Board Meeting of which I am a member. We recently faced very considerable and untrue calumny. Of course we cannot avoid the reality that any effective and pertinent mission must expect definite opposition – unfruitful work which cuts no ice is not worth opposing. But we were confronted with libellous and scurrilous defamation which had no basis in truth. Should we follow the example of Jesus in his trial and crucifixion? Should we remain silent, not refute the accusations and trust that the attacks would die down and be forgotten? Or should we follow the earlier path of Jesus and denounce those who were opposing us? Should we defend ourselves and even take our opponents to court so that our honesty as Christians might be vindicated? The mission felt it right and Christ-like to take the latter course and start legal procedures.

We faced a similar situation at All Nations Christian College some thirty years ago. At that time the college was just beginning to become better known as a leader in mission training; but our good reputation was still not firmly established or widely acknowledged. We had invited a Russian Orthodox priest and a leading Roman Catholic to give a couple of lectures. One Christian paper contained a scurrilous editorial denouncing All Nations as a college which encouraged its students to worship icons and to dance before statues of Mary. Various supporters of the college offered to write letters in our defence, but the principal at that time declined their offers. He based his approach on the model of Jesus who remained silent when falsely accused and did not open his mouth to defend himself.

In these two parallel cases we see two Christian movements seeking to follow the pattern of Jesus in his reactions to his opponents. Yet they differed totally in their response. In different situations at different stages in his life and ministry Jesus reacts to his enemies in different ways. As his followers we have to ask ourselves which model in the life of Jesus fits our situation most appropriately. And we need constantly to examine our motives to check that pride, anger or self-aggrieved hurt do not underlie our response.

In our desire to be loving and gracious, Christians can tend only to emphasize Jesus' meekness and humility, remaining silent before his accusers. But we should not forget that Jesus is not always quiet when under attack. Sometimes he even counter-attacks and denounces his enemies.

In Matthew 21:23–27 Jesus is faced with an aggressive trick question: 'By what authority are you doing these things? Who gave you this authority?' Jesus not only fails to give a direct answer, but reverses the whole situation by asking his inquisitors another question. Thus Jesus sets us a model of how to deal with dishonest trick questions. It is often unwise to give a straight answer. It may be better to counter with a related question of our own which places the discussion on more positive ground.

In Matthew 21:28–32 Jesus counter-attacks with the story of the two sons:

'There was a man who had two sons. He went to the first and said, "Son, go and work today in the vineyard." "I will not," he answered, but later he changed his mind and went. Then the father went to the other son and said the same thing. He answered, "I will, sir," but he did not go. Which of the two did what his father wanted?' 'The first,' they answered. Jesus said to them, 'I tell you the truth, the tax collectors and the prostitutes are entering the kingdom of God ahead of you. For John came to you to show you the way of righteousness, and you did not believe him, but the tax collectors and the prostitutes did. And even after you saw this, you did not repent and believe him.'

Jesus then tells the further parable of the tenants, showing the fearful sin that they are involved in and will be involved in. He warns them of the judgement that will come upon them as a result, and he does not mince his words. We find likewise with the later Herod that Jesus in Luke 13 calls him 'that fox' – hardly British politeness. There is sometimes a danger that those used to British culture, which is gracious, polite and 'softly softly', don't understand the New Testament culture, which is often brutally direct. Jesus himself therefore can sound very confrontational in his dealings with his opponents. Expressions like 'that fox' and 'whitened sepulchres' hardly relate to what we learn in modern British missiology. On the other hand, some contemporary Jewish missions can seem very direct and upfront.

Forgiveness

This discussion of Jesus' opponents leads us to the difficult but vital question of whether as Christians we are called to forgive those who oppose or abuse us even when they do not repent of their evil. Are we called upon to forgive, even if there is no repentance? Once again we should remind ourselves that in all things our attitudes are to follow the model of Jesus and the character of God the Father. We have therefore to ask how God relates to unrepentant sinners. We believe also that Jesus Christ gives us the perfect mirror image of the Father, so we also need to note Jesus' attitude to his enemies.

In the New Testament, God's gracious forgiveness in Jesus Christ is always conditional on human repentance. In his absolute holiness God cannot 'behold evil' (Hab. 1:13). He cannot relate to sin. Divine judgement must prevail where persistence in sin rejects God's offer of forgiveness and a new relationship with him. Repentance is essential before the atoning work of Jesus Christ can be appreciated.

Yet God longs to forgive everyone, and holds out the offer of forgiveness to all without discrimination. John's Gospel underlines the truth that God loves 'the world', not only his own covenant people. John 3:16 declares that God's love is universal; but his saving gift of eternal life has the precondition of faith – and New Testament faith is linked inseparably to repentance. So we must distinguish carefully between God's love and God's forgiveness. They are closely interrelated, but they are not coextensive. His love shines upon all; and his forgiveness is offered to all, but cannot be completed unless repentance is present.

Turning to Jesus' example, we notice a further aspect. In the context of the Roman soldiers having nailed him to the cross (Lk. 23:32–34) Jesus prayed, 'Father, forgive them, because they do not know what they are doing.' These men were acting in obedience to their officers, without specific malicious intent or hatred towards Jesus. In their eyes he was just another criminal and they had to do their duty. Praying for them in this way, Jesus showed his longing for their forgiveness and his own willingness not to hold anything against them. We notice that he did not specifically state that this forgiveness depended on their repentance; but his prayer would never have flouted his Father's laws. In this action Jesus was modelling that it is right to offer forgiveness to those who have little or no understanding of what they are doing against us. Of all Jesus' enemies on that fateful Good Friday these soldiers were the least culpable.

But what about those who deliberately and spitefully ill-treat us? The Jewish leaders and Pilate fall into this category. It is striking how the various disparate groups in the society of Jesus' day united in opposition against him. In normal times the Sadducees and Pharisees sat in opposite corners of the ring and Herod and the Romans had little regard for either party. Romans and Jews despised each other. But in the final period of Jesus' life, and for his crucifixion, every group was united in opposition to him. All of these showed no indication of repentance and therefore God's judgement rested on them. And this judgement fell, not only on these guilty individuals, but also corporately on Israel, and Jerusalem, and later on Rome whose administration put Jesus on the cross.

The unfolding story also shows us the fickle crowds. They did not realize the significance of what they were doing, but they were guilty in that they allowed themselves to be incited to complicity in the unjust and criminal evil which took place. Matthew calls the leaders 'the elders of the people' to indicate that the leaders and the people shared together in guilt. The crowds had not initiated the crime, so their guilt was less. But they too would need to repent before they could be forgiven. Therefore Peter's first sermon on the day of Pentecost climaxed in a challenge for all to repent.

Despite the horrifying evil of the crucifixion, God still loved everyone concerned and offered them his forgiveness bought by the death of Christ. But where there was no repentance, God's judgement fell. And so today his loving grace is available to Israel and all the world, but his forgiveness cannot be received unless there is repentance.

As followers of God in Christ we too are called to love all people unconditionally, however evil they may be in opposing, misusing and even abusing us. Love believes and hopes all things, 1 Corinthians 13 tells us. Love therefore sees the potential for good in those who do evil to us; it longs for them to come to repentance and such new life as will liberate them from the power, guilt and burden of sin. Following the beautiful model of God the Father, love has wide open arms which are waiting in expectant hope to run out to welcome the repentant sinner, to embrace and forgive them, to enter with rejoicing into a new relationship with them.

Like God, then, we are called to love our enemies. Such love eagerly desires to forgive. Indeed, following God's example, it holds out the offer of forgiveness to its persecutors. But their receiving forgiveness depends on their repentance. As weak and sinful human beings we constantly face the danger of allowing our personal hurts to engender bitterness and cloud our love. While God does not forgive the unrepentant, he never allows bitterness into his heart. Unholy anger, self-centred bitterness and hurt pride may be very normal in human society, but they are not God-like and they poison our relationships so that love becomes impossible. It is not at all easy to maintain a genuine holy love without bitterness, but that is part of God's pattern and must be our goal in our attitude towards those who stand against us and remain unrepentant.

The model that we are aiming for is surely the model of Jesus in his reactions to his opponents and his enemies: loving, and yet realistic, facing the reality of hatred and opposition. He denounced that opposition, warning of the woes and the judgement that will be their portion. Jesus does indeed clearly warn of the reality of judgement, and the 'woe passages' (e.g. Mt. 23:13–39) are significant in this. He clearly declares that the kingdom will be taken away from those leaders who oppose him, but he continues steadily to pursue his calling and his ministry, including his death, as God's purpose for the salvation of the world. And in the midst of it all, he continues to be open in love to anyone, including those groups which bitterly opposed him. His arms of love reached out to anyone who would seek him. He also felt grief and compassion for the crowds and for the oppressed, the marginalized and the poor. He is our model, and we follow him.

4

Jesus' Relationships with Jews, Samaritans and Gentiles

In looking at Jesus' relationships with Jews, Samaritans and Gentiles it may prove helpful to remind ourselves of the context of the New Testament, the context in which Jesus was living. Jesus was, of course, a Jew: he was indeed incarnate as a particular Jew at a particular time. It was a time when Jews looked down on Gentiles and considered them godless and immoral. But by the time the gospels were written, Jesus was largely rejected by most of his own people, and that raised questions both in the church and outside the church. It led to serious questions in criticism of the church. Was Jesus actually a failure? How can he be the Messiah of Israel when his own people generally reject him?

At the same time large numbers of Gentiles were pressing into the church and becoming followers of the Jewish Jesus. This raised the question whether it was right for Gentiles to be followers of Jesus. Was it right that a Gentile could become a follower of the God of Israel and of the Jewish Messiah without becoming a proselyte or even a God-fearer? Should not Gentile converts be circumcised and follow the Jewish Law, becoming part of Israel as in the Old Testament times? In the Old Testament proselytes had to join themselves to the people of Israel, if they were going to become followers of the God of Israel. And so there were radical questions concerning the universality of the gospel. These were issues which concerned the life of the church and its mission.

In the early days of the Christian Church it was comfortably Jewish with no inter-ethnic or cross-cultural problems. Then the early church began to face problems. Christians had to struggle with the issue of fellowship and harmony together in a multi-cultural church with members from very different backgrounds. The New Testament witnesses to the development of a mixed church with Jews and Gentiles together, and not only a mixed church with the two together, but actually a church in which the Jewish majority fairly rapidly became a minority. The church was largely taken over by the now Gentile majority. So, the church had to face questions of how to live together as Jews and Gentiles. This is particularly addressed in the first church council, as recorded in Acts 15. Paul also teaches about it in Romans 14 and 15, and in Colossians.

The difficult situation they faced is sometimes mirrored today. In many parts of the world it may happen that congregations find themselves swamped and taken over by Christians of a different cultural or ethnic background. Older and more traditional church members are forced to yield to the younger generation. For instance, in Singapore we watched older Chinese-speaking churches having to give way to younger English-speaking Chinese Christians whose culture was less traditional and more cosmopolitan.

As we have seen, something parallel took place in the history of the British Seventh Day Adventist churches. Some years ago they had approximately 10,000 members, who were almost exclusively white and ethnically English. Then there was an influx of black Afro-Caribbeans, who were not just immature new Christians, quite a few of them had been in leadership in their previous churches. Some had even been pastors. So, as they came into the Seventh Day Adventist churches they took many of them over. Suddenly the Seventh Day Adventists had a majority of black pastors and the whole character of the church changed. A black style of worship was introduced, which was very different from the traditional English. This went together with a black style of preaching, of fellowship and community. Indeed the whole cultural background changed in many of the congregations. Many of the whites could not adapt. Of the 10,000 members, some 5,000 left. But at the same time about 10,000 blacks joined, so the church grew and the 10,000 became approximately 15,000. Something parallel happened as the early Jewish churches were increasingly taken over by the new Gentile Christians.

In Europe today our problem concerning Jews and Gentiles has been exacerbated by some of the Reformation translations of the Scriptures in the various European languages. Thus, in French, German, and Scandinavian languages the word for 'Gentile' is commonly translated by the word for 'pagan' or 'heathen'. In French it is '*les paiens*'; in German it is '*die Heiden*'. Such translations change the sense of the word from one of ethnicity to one of faith. The Gentiles are now understood not as the 'non-Jews', but as the non-Christian 'pagans'. Thus, Thomas Aquinas wrote a major work called 'Contra Gentiles'/'Against the Gentiles' in which he describes the non-Christian Jews as 'Gentiles' while the Gentile European Christians are 'the new Israel'! In this way the sense of Scripture is perverted. Likewise the early Puritan missionaries called the North American Indians 'Gentiles' while applying the biblical promises concerning Israel to themselves although they were actually Gentiles too.

When introducing my wife in a meeting, I sometimes mention that she is Gentile. I have had people come to me afterwards to complain, 'How can you say such a thing about your wife? That's dreadful! Publicly to denigrate her in that way!' I then have to explain that to be Gentile is purely a fact of ethnicity. It is neither positive nor pejorative. There are Jews, and there are Gentiles – and when the New Testament is talking about Jews and Gentiles we need to bear that in mind.

It is in the context of racial identity that the Gospels emphasize Jesus' relationships with the Gentiles. In the previous chapter we looked briefly at the Nazareth synagogue reading in Luke chapter 4, but we now note that these verses lead on immediately into the reality of God's grace which Isaiah foretells and which Luke 4 refers to.

This grace applies to Gentiles as well as Jews. At the conclusion of the synagogue reading in Luke 4:18, 19, Luke comments that 'Jesus then rolled up the scroll, gave it back to the attendant and sat down. And the eyes of everyone in the synagogue were fastened on him.' They were wondering why he finished reading where he did. Who was this Jesus who curtailed the reading without completing what is said in Isaiah 61? They concluded, however, that his action demonstrated his grace. And so, in v. 22: 'All spoke well of him and were amazed at the words of grace that came from his lips.' Jesus was showing that grace not only applies to Jews, and particularly to the poor and the prisoners, but grace relates also to Gentiles because he does not go on to read the words in the second half of Isaiah 61. These verses (Isa. 61:5ff.) reflect the typical Old Testament view that the salvation of Israel is linked with the judgement of the Gentiles. He then continues in Luke. 4:24, 'I tell you the truth, no prophet is accepted in his home area. I assure you that there were many widows in Israel in Elijah's time; yet Elijah was not sent to any of them, but to a widow in Zarephath in the region of Sidon,' a Gentile woman. And 'there were many in Israel with leprosy in the time of Elisha the prophet, yet not one of them was cleansed, only

Naaman the Syrian.' The people in the synagogue were furi-
ous when they heard this – they were good Jews, and this
denigration of Jesus' own Jewish people in favour of the
Gentiles was infuriating to that Jewish community and they
tried to kill him. They still had not learned that God's election of Israel as his particular people did not preclude the
fact that his grace is also for Gentiles of every race and background.

In the previous chapter we also looked briefly at
Matthew chapter 8, which recounts how Jesus had authority over the wind and the waves. We did not at that stage
elaborate on the fact that Jesus then went across the lake to
the area of Gadara, to the area of the Gadarene people on
the east side of the lake. The Gadarenes were Gentiles, so
Jesus was moving into a Gentile area. In 'The Biblical Foundations for Mission' (SCM 1983) D. Senior and C.
Stuhlmueller in the chapter on Mark's Gospel rightly com-
ment that when Jesus moves into a Gentile area there is
always demonic opposition. Jesus has to withstand
demonic attack when he moves into the realm of the
Gentiles and outside that of his own Jewish people. So
Mark emphasizes the ferocity of the storm and the opposition of the demonic powers in the Gadarene man. To show
that this event relates to Gentiles rather than Jews, Mark
recounts how the demons ended up in pigs which is in
Jewish thought where demons belong!

We may also observe in the gospels that Jesus is very
much at home in Galilee in contrast to Jerusalem and Judea.
Galilee is the centre of his ministry; that is also where he
meets his disciples following the resurrection. And Galilee,
as Matthew points out, is indeed 'Galilee of the Gentiles'
(Mt. 4:15). Of course there were also a lot of Jews living in
Galilee; it was a mixed race area, but there was a majority of
Gentiles, which is why it was called 'Galilee of the Gentiles'.

But in spite of the fact that Jesus throughout his ministry is opening the door for God's grace to reach out also to Gentiles, he remains involved primarily with his own people. We must never forget that Jesus and his disciples were Jews; they were not Gentiles.

While it is true that Jesus' ministry among Gentiles does open the door in preparation for the church's wider outreach to people of all nations, he is by no means implying a form of anti-semitic replacement theology. Replacement theology has taught that God's election in the Old Testament was focussed on the Jews as the people of Israel, but that in the New Testament era of grace God replaced the Jews and his light shone on the Gentiles. Only in the end times, they have taught, would God bring Jews back into his kingdom. Such a theology not only presents considerable problems to Jewish Christians now, who seem to have become believers at the wrong time in history, before the so-called future 'end time'; it also appears to be contrary to the teaching of the New Testament.

Although in Acts 13:46 Paul and Barnabas boldly proclaimed that they would now 'turn to the Gentiles', in the immediately following events they continued to preach in 'the Jewish synagogue' (Acts 14:1) with the result that a large number both of Jews and of Greeks believed. The church does not become Gentile to the neglect of Jewish believers, but rather begins its progress towards universality with Jews and Gentiles of all nations as its members. Evangelization of Jews remains a Christian priority still today, but not to the exclusion of concern also for Gentiles of all nations.

In some New Testament scholarship today John's gospel is particularly singled out for criticism as being anti-semitic because of its often negative approach to 'the Jews'. There is considerable debate concerning the meaning in John's gospel of 'the Jews' – 'Judaioi' could refer to

Judaeans and we know from the gospels that Judea and Jerusalem were the centre of opposition to Jesus. Was John therefore referring to the leaders of the Jews in Judea who so strongly attacked and finally caused the crucifixion of Jesus? Certainly S. Motyer (*Your Father the Devil? A new approach to John and "the Jews"*, Paternoster 1997) convincingly refutes the critical accusations of anti-semitism in John's gospel.

Perhaps it needs also to be remembered that most peoples can sometimes be strongly critical of their own people. Thus the British are often quite negative in what they say about their own people and likewise Anglican Christians can be the harshest critics of their own denomination. Jews too among themselves can sound quite anti-semitic, although they would feel offended if Gentiles would utter such negative things about Jews. So it may be that what sounds anti-semitic in the New Testament represents only typical in-house criticism. Again we must not forget that the New Testament (with the possible exception of Luke, although that too is debatable) is written by Jews and therefore the charge of anti-semitism is unlikely to be well-founded despite the rejection of Jesus and the Christian Church by the great majority of Jews.

Of course it is true that the synoptic gospels also stress that the kingdom will be taken away from Israel and given to a new 'laos', a new people. That people will be universal, not just Jews. The kingdom will therefore no longer be centred on Israel as God's particular elect and chosen people, but will now be widened to all who believe in Jesus, Jew and Gentile of all races.

Despite, therefore, what is often popularly and unthinkingly stated, Pentecost is not the birthday of the church. The New Testament word used for the church 'ekklēsia' is merely the Greek translation of the Hebrew 'qahal', one of the words used in the Old Testament for 'the congregation' of Israel. There is a direct continuity from God's people as the congregation of Israel to the universal church of God. The qahal/ekklēsia now consists of all who believe in Jesus Christ, whether Jew or Gentile. Not only Jews, but all can now become God's children (Jn. 1:12).

Jesus points out again and again the marvellous reality of Gentiles' faith in contrast to the unbelief of many of his people at that time. It seems in his humanity that this surprises him. Jesus was incarnate as a human being, and as such he has human reactions. It was indeed very natural that he should be surprised that Jews could possibly reject their own Messiah and that Gentiles could have such amazing openness of faith. He marvels and points it out on several occasions, noting the reality of Gentiles' faith in contrast to the hard-hearted unbelief of many Jews at that time. He thus rebukes the lack of faith of so many Jews. Sadly this re-action is still true for those of us who are Jewish Christians, working for Jesus Christ among our own people. We too need sometimes to rebuke our own people for their lack of faith, and sometimes we are amazed at their blindness. Likewise it sometimes amazes us as Jewish Christians how perceptive and how faithful Gentile Christians can be.

Nevertheless, in spite of such emphases in the New Testament, Jesus did relate particularly to his own people, to the Jews. Indeed, he declares that he was sent particularly to the lost sheep of the house of Israel (Mt. 15:24). He restricted his ministry largely to within the borders of Israel and in relationship to his own people. He still needed to fulfil the Old Testament calling which ministered specially to Israel, while at the same time acting as a magnet to draw the Gentiles in. He is the climactic summit of the Old Testament, to which everything in the Old Testament is pointing. Only when the Old Testament has come to its climactic fulfilment can the door be opened for the wider ministry to the Gentiles. For this reason Jesus ministers largely within the borders of Israel and in relationship to his own people. Likewise he chose Jewish people as his twelve disciples with all the significance of that number twelve – I always smile at the fact that he chose Jewish disciples when some of the people who oppose women's leadership in the church point out that Jesus only had men as leaders, and as disciples! Is it only men who should be ordained? The only disciples Jesus had were Jews, so logically the only people who should be ordained in the Church are Jews and we should defrock all the Gentiles! That might however cause something of a disaster in the Christian Church, and some consternation!

Jesus' special relationship to his own people is a model for us and in our vocation to mission we must also not forget our own people. It is easy for those of us who are called into mission to Africa, Asia, the Middle East, or Latin America to become much more interested in other peoples than in our own home nation and people. We have in Christ a pattern of deep, heartfelt concern and relationship with our own people, but it must also maintain the wider universal mission vision. It should not be blinkered or exclusive.

The Samaritans

We now move on from the Jews to the Samaritans. Before we can consider Jesus' relationship to the Gentiles we need to look at the New Testament which stresses for us the bridge between the Jews and the Gentiles, namely the Samaritans. This bridge may be seen in the book of Acts e.g. Acts 1:8, the text on which the book of Acts is built, 'But you will receive power when the Holy Spirit has come upon you, *and* you shall be my witnesses in Jerusalem and all Judea, and Samaria and to the ends of the earth.' The word 'and' demonstrates the inseparable connection of the power of the Holy Spirit together with worldwide witness. The

Samaritans form a half-way house between witness to Jews and to Gentiles. The Samaritans developed as a people from mixed marriages between Jews and those Gentiles who had been settled in Israel to occupy the depopulated land after Israel's exile to Babylon. In their religion they revered the first five books of the Bible, they worshipped the same creator God as the Jews, but worshipped at a temple on Mount Gerizim not in Jerusalem, and they looked to Moses as the Restorer who was to return. The Samaritans were then a mixture of Jewish and Gentile elements, thus forming a natural bridge from the Jewish into the Gentile world.

Acts 1–7 is concerned exclusively with Jewish mission with a few proselytes added to the people of God. It basically tells the story of witness to Jerusalem and all Judea. Thus Pentecost was a Jewish experience – but Gentile believers are now also welcome to the fullness of the Holy Spirit!

The structure of the Book of Acts demonstrates the actual outworking of the Jews-Samaritans-Gentiles order which we have already observed in Acts 1:8. Between the Jewish mission section in chapters 1–7 and the conversion in chapter 9 of Paul, the apostle to the Gentiles, Luke places two intermediate bridges. In Acts 8:1–25 mission among the Samaritans is highlighted. But the Samaritans are not the only stepping stone to a wider development of the church into Gentile circles. The second half of Acts 8 recounts the conversion of the Ethiopian eunuch. Although this man was a Gentile, he was also a God-fearer who was worshipping the God of Israel in the temple of Israel. Indeed he was also reading the scriptures of Israel in the book of Isaiah. So he joins the Samaritans as a further bridge into the Gentile world. Only after Acts 8 does Luke tell of Paul's conversion and then the apostolic outreach to the Gentiles.

God is gracious and gentle in the way he leads his disciples into new avenues of ministry. He does not parachute

them into radical or unacceptable service. Rather he takes
them gradually step by step into such untrodden territory
For Jewish Christians in the first century to venture directly
into mission among Gentiles would have been unthinkable.
So the Spirit of Jesus introduces them first to the intermediate stage of witness to the Samaritans and the God-fearing
Ethiopian.

Returning from the Acts of the Apostles to the Gospels
we see how Jesus had already in his lifetime broken down
the disciples' prejudice against the Samaritans. In AD 7 some
Samaritans had come to Jerusalem and defiled the Holy of
Holies in the Temple by scattering dead animals there. Such
an offensive sacrilegious act must have introduced considerable antipathy into Jew-Samaritan relationships, although the then Herod had worked hard to reconcile these
two peoples within his realm. It is noteworthy that the boy
Jesus must have been presented at the Temple in Jerusalem
at about that time or shortly afterwards. At such an impres-
sionable age he must have felt the atmosphere of embittered
relationships and indeed it is emphasized that 'Jews do not
associate with Samaritans' (Jn. 4:9). It is all the more remarkable how he purposefully stresses the place of the Samaritans within the purposes of God's kingdom. This not
only introduces his disciples to a wider mission perspective,
but also demonstrates how in Jesus' own life he models a
reconciliation which breaks down all barriers. No longer is
being a Samaritan equivalent in the eyes of Jesus' followers
to being demon-possessed (c.f. Jn. 8:48).

So we see Jesus making a point of relating to the Samaritans. Thus he heals ten lepers, but only one returns to give
him thanks. The punch-line of the story is 'and he was a
Samaritan' (Lk. 17:16) which goes together with Jesus'
words 'your faith has made you well' (Lk. 17:19); so saving
faith is not the sole prerogative of Jews. Samaritans can also
be saved through faith in Jesus.

Jesus also tells the well-known parable of the Good Samaritan. This story is often inadequately understood in our Christian churches, as if it merely taught that people should give assistance to the poor and needy. Clearly the parable does teach us to be good neighbours in loving and helping people in distress, but it is also emphasizing that it was a Samaritan who proved to be the good neighbour. It is in this way a radical story. Jesus' parable might have surprised a Jewish audience if it had told of a Jew who helped a Samaritan – Jews strongly believe in charitable giving, but this is largely restricted to those in need within the Jewish community. The parable shocks its hearers even more by declaring that the Jew in need was not helped by the leaders of his own people, but by a generous Samaritan.

Pride sometimes prevents Christians today from allowing the possibility that we might need outside help. Some years ago I mentioned in a talk that the large fast-growing churches of Indonesia would have much to teach us in the British church. Afterwards I was shocked to receive an indignant letter from a well-known English pastor in which he wrote, 'We have NO (I repeat: NO) need of ANY (I repeat: ANY) help from ANY (I repeat: ANY) church overseas.' Of course we can sympathize with the reaction against accounts of church growth in Korea or America which imply that if our churches adopted their style wholesale we would automatically share their success. Nevertheless Paul's teaching concerning the body of Christ remains true. No member may dare to say of another member, 'I don't need you' (1 Cor. 12:12ff). The British church needs other churches; Jews need the Samaritans. Samaritans also play a vital role within the kingdom.

When the time was ripe, Jesus left his beloved Galilee and set his face to go up to Jerusalem. Instead of following the long route down the Mediterranean coast he went direct through Samaria and thus risked the accusation of ritual uncleanness as he passed through the Samaritan villages. It is recorded that these villages rejected him 'because he was heading for Jerusalem' (Lk. 9:53). If he had intended to worship at the Samaritan shrine, he would have been welcomed by them. Likewise if he had by-passed Samaria on his way to Jerusalem, the Jews might have approved. But to go to Jerusalem through Samaria was provocatively un-diplomatic – Jesus' pattern does not always fit the British desire for wise tactfulness!

Evidently Jesus' disciples had still not learned their lesson. They still regarded the Samaritans with antipathy and did not yet share Jesus' universal vision for all peoples. Lacking that missionary love for their Samaritan neigh-bours, they asked Jesus, 'Lord, do you want us to call fire down from heaven to destroy them?' (Lk. 9:54) But gradu-ally Jesus' attitude to the Samaritans did break through and in Acts 8 the apostles needed no special guidance to encourage them to preach to the Samaritans.

Jesus' most remarkable incident in his relationship to the Samaritans comes in John 4. While this conversation be-tween Jesus and the Samaritan woman is sometimes used in more conservative Christian circles to teach how to witness on a one-to-one basis, John and his readers would surely have observed a deeper significance. Although many of the leading Jewish rabbis realized that the Old Testament taught that God's kingdom was universal and not just for Israel, the common assumption remained that the kingdom of heaven was for three sorts of people. It was for Jews, not for Gentiles or Samaritans unless they joined themselves to the people of Israel as proselytes through circumcision and submission to the Law/Torah. It was also for men, not for women who were not allowed to study Torah. Finally it was for good, pious Jewish men whose faith in God and Torah issued in obedience and good works in accordance with the Law. So it is radically significant that Jesus reveals himself so clearly and unequivocally as the long-expected Messiah (Jn. 4:25, 26) in this particular remarkable incident. John underlines the word 'the woman' in his account (Jn. 4: 9, 11, 15, 19, 21, 25, 27, 28, 39, 42). He also carefully shows that she had had five 'husbands' and indeed that her present partner was not her husband (4:17, 18), so she must have been known locally for her immorality. And of course she was a Samaritan, not a Jew or proselyte. In this way Jesus contradicts the popular view of the kingdom of God and demonstrates his loving concern for all people – for men and women, for sinners and not just for the righteous, for Samaritans as well as for Jews. Jesus desires to relate widely in his kingdom.

So Jesus in his ministry on earth related specifically to the Samaritans and thus opened the door for his followers to preach the gospel to all people everywhere. Samaritans and Gentiles can now be accepted into the embrace of his saving love.

As we have already mentioned, Jesus' relationship with Samaritans shows his gracious patience in leading his disciples gradually one step at a time into a wider, international understanding of the church. Still today in our weakness we need Jesus to take us by the hand and bring us gently into deeper commitment and a wider vision.

For example, a few years ago I was asked to speak at an international conference for Messianic Jewish leaders. I chose to expound the Book of Acts and showed how the Holy Spirit has called us as Jewish believers in Jesus to reach out in evangelism not only to our own people, but also to Gentiles all over the world. Various of those attending the conference made it very clear to me that such a message was not acceptable. Stressing Paul's teaching on the priority of mission 'to the Jews first', they felt that we should concentrate on work within the Jewish community and indeed that the primary task of Gentile Christians should be centred on the Jewish people. While it is true in the New Testament that mission among Jews does have some form of priority (it is not appropriate here to discuss the various Christian interpretations of what this priority means), it was evidently not easy for these particular Messianic leaders to widen their horizons.

Some Gentile British Christians can sometimes hold to an equally blinkered outlook. Racial pride easily prevails in a way which reminds us of the old song 'The English, the English, the English are best; I wouldn't give tuppence for all of the rest.' So our churches are often ethnically exclusive with little or no regard for other cultures in spite of globalization and the ethnic diversity which has come to almost all nations. God may need gently to break this pattern by introducing one or two rather westernized African or Asian Christians of maturity into the congregation. When the white British Christians have become used to these first ethnically different members, they may then be able to begin to relate to others from the ethnic minorities in their neighbourhood and adjust to such cross-cultural mission.

European young people in our increasingly post-modern cultures find it very hard to contemplate long-term commitment to mission overseas. They are happy to go abroad on a short mission trip for a couple of weeks or perhaps even to spend some nine months overseas in their 'gap year' between school and university. Many more seasoned overseas workers complain about this trend to short-term mission. They know from experience that short-term workers lack time to adapt culturally beyond superficial externals, to walk in the sandals of the new world-view, to learn the local language and make deep personal relationships. But even in this God leads his people one step at a time. Short-term workers can become more committed long-term missionaries. 'Little tigers become big tigers', the Asian proverb declares.

So Jesus' relationship with Samaritans gave the disciples a wider perspective and prepared the way for the more difficult calling of mission to the Gentiles. Because of Jesus' example, by Acts 8 they had learned their lesson and needed no direct guidance from God before they were willing to preach to the Samaritans. But mission to the Gentiles required a further step and was still not easy for them.

The Gentiles

In the Book of Acts Luke dedicates almost two whole chapters to the conversion of Cornelius, the beginning of wider mission also to Gentiles. Peter is unprepared for this major move towards Gentile mission until God gives him the vision of both kosher and non-kosher animals let down on a sheet from heaven. Peter resists the command to kill and eat, but the voice from heaven warns him against calling anything unclean which God has cleansed. Then the Gentile messengers arrive, and it dawns on Peter that these people who he had considered unclean are actually clean in God's sight. So he goes with them to the very house of the Gentile, Cornelius.

In this story we not only observe how the Spirit of Jesus is breaking down the Jewish prejudice against the Gentiles and prodding Peter into a new willingness to relate to the Gentiles. We also note a transition from the Old Testament pattern of mission to that of the New Testament.

In the Old Testament Israel was not sent out to the Gentile nations to preach the message of God, but was called to reflect and demonstrate God's glory and holiness with the aim that the Gentiles might see, believe and come in to Jerusalem to worship the God of Israel. The life of Israel both corporately as God's people and individually was to act as a magnet to draw the Gentiles to God, like honey attracting bees. Only in the New Testament was the church sent out into the world to preach. Mission thus began as a centripetal force and only after Christ's death added the centrifugal movement. So in Acts 10 and 11 Gentiles first come in to Peter in Old Testament fashion and then Peter goes out to the Gentiles with a New Testament pattern of mission.

It was not only Peter who still needed a forceful call from God to make him willing to go to the Gentiles in mission. Paul too did not find this an easy step. In Antioch of Pisidia Paul and Barnabas experienced from the Jewish population rejection and fierce opposition to the message of Jesus. But many Gentiles responded willingly with faith. The combination of Jewish unbelief and Gentile openness moved Paul to enter into the calling he had received at his conversion to be the apostle to the Gentiles. So in Acts 13:46 he boldly declares the crucial words 'we now turn to the Gentiles' and supports this with a vital quotation from Isaiah 49:6:

'I have made you a light for the Gentiles, that you may bring salvation to the ends of the earth.'

So how far had Jesus prepared his followers for this huge change of perspective which was going to be demanded of them? In his earthly ministry Jesus had prepared his followers for witness to Samaritans and, as we have seen, after the resurrection and Pentecost they moved into that ministry without questioning its validity. But Jesus' approach to the Gentiles during his incarnate ministry was not so unequivocal and therefore the apostles required a more definite initiative from God to convince them of the rightness of mission among Gentiles.

In the light of their experience of the influx of Gentiles into the early church the gospel writers looked back to the life of Jesus and remembered how he had taught about the

Gentiles and how he had related to them. So Luke not only tells of Jesus going through Samaritan villages on his way to Jerusalem, but sees too how this incident relates to wider Gentile mission. It comes just after the sending out of the twelve and introduces Jesus' sending out of the seventy (Lk. 10:1).

In Jewish thought the number twelve clearly refers to Israel and the number seventy was used to refer to the Gentiles because it was the number of the children of Noah through Shem, Ham and Japheth. Noah was considered to be the father of all peoples and it is accepted that the Noachic covenant is for Gentiles as well as for Israel. It should be noted however that there are variant manuscript readings for Luke 10:1 in which some cite the number seventy and others change to seventy-two. It is relevant here to say that the same is true of the number of elders involved in the translation of the Septuagint, the first Gentile language translation of the Hebrew scriptures. These debates concerning Luke 10:1 and the Septuagint reflect an early rabbinic argument as to whether the correct number for the Gentiles is seventy or seventy-two.

So Luke is showing Jesus progressing from the sending of the twelve to a widening of his ministry to include Samaritans, who in their turn are a stepping stone towards the sending out of the seventy/seventy-two. Jesus is extending the vision of his disciples to include also the Gentiles.

It is significant that in Luke 9 between the Samaritan incident and the sending out of the seventy/seventy-two Luke introduces Jesus' challenging interaction with three men (Lk. 9:57–62). The cost of following Jesus is underlined, for Jesus 'has no place to lay his head'. To follow him as their rabbi even meant giving discipleship of Jesus priority over the demands of family and over the burying of the dead. The ministry of the seventy/seventy-two and by implication Gentile mission involves such sacrifice and suffering that

Jesus needed to warn his followers that 'no one who puts their hand to the plough and looks back is fit for service in the kingdom of God.' Only then did he send the seventy/ seventy-two to prepare the way for his coming. Like John the Baptist they were to be forerunners before the king who wanted to come not only to Israel and to the Samaritans, but also now to the Gentiles. The harvest would prove plentiful (Lk. 10:2), but the workers would be inadequately few – perhaps because of the sacrificial cost of this calling. Jesus calls his people therefore to pray that God would 'send out workers into his harvest field'; the word translated 'send out' is a violent term which literally means 'throw out' and it implies that people may be naturally unwilling for the sacrificial service of mission among Gentiles and therefore need to be 'kicked out'!

Although Jesus specifically states that he was sent to the lost sheep of Israel (Mt. 15:24), all the gospel writers stress the beginnings of a wider ministry of Jesus Christ, not only to Jews or Samaritans, but also to Gentiles. With the increasing influx of Gentiles into the church and the violent rejection of Jesus as Messiah by most Jews urgent questions pressed for answers. Were Christians mistaken in their faith in Jesus as Lord and Saviour? Was there a precedent in the life of Jesus himself for opposition from most of the Jewish people and for the acceptance of Gentiles as followers of Jesus?

The gospels honestly show something of the Jewish negativity towards the Gentiles. That is reflected even in the New Testament. For example in Matthew 6:32 Jesus asks, 'What shall we eat, and what shall we wear?' He then says that the Gentiles run after all these things. But you are not like the Gentiles; you do not need to be anxious about material things, for your heavenly Father knows that you need them. These verses are a bit negative about Gentiles. Likewise, in Luke 18:32 that same negativity towards the

Gentiles is seen. It is to the Gentiles that Jesus will be handed over. They will mock and insult him, spit on him, flog him and kill him. Again and again in the gospels we note such reflections of Jewish negativity towards Gentiles. When Jesus is teaching about Christian leadership, he says, 'The Gentiles lord it over their people, but it shall not be so among you.' You expect Gentiles to be authoritarian; that is a typically Gentile form of leadership – and it is reprehensible. It shall not be so among you however. You are not to be like the Gentiles, Jesus says to his disciples.

In that context of negativity it is particularly significant how Jesus relates to the Gentiles. Of course Jesus stands in continuity with the background of Old Testament injunctions with regard to justice for the aliens within Israel's gates and care for foreigners, including slaves and servants of other ethnic backgrounds. But Jesus goes further in his relationship to the Gentiles. He breaks down the barriers between races and peoples, in giving us a model for our community and social lives as well as our church lives in the modern day. He reaches out to people of all races with his grace and his mercy.

Let us look particularly at one passage in Matthew as an example. In Matthew 14:13–21 Jesus feeds the crowd of 5,000 men. It was evidently a Jewish crowd. We observe that the disciples took the initiative in going to Jesus in v. 15: 'As evening approached the disciples came to Jesus and they said, "This is a remote place and it's already getting late. Send the crowds away so that they can go to the villages and buy themselves some food." ' They were concerned for the welfare of the Jewish crowds, although their initiative was somewhat ambivalent. Their commendable concern was rather spoiled by the suggestion: 'Send the crowds away' – the same words they were later to say with reference to a Gentile woman (Mt. 15:23). On the contrary, when they are faced with the Gentile crowd of 4,000 men, it

is Jesus who takes the initiative. He calls his disciples to him
and says, 'I have compassion for these people, they've already been with me three days and have nothing to eat. I
don't want to send them away hungry or they may collapse
on the way' (Mt. 15:32). So Jesus is again showing his disciples that he has compassion, not just on Jewish crowds, but
also on the Gentiles.

In the feeding both of the Jewish and the Gentile crowds
Jesus uses his disciples. He did not need their assistance, but
in his grace he uses and thus also trains his disciples in his
service. This also gives them a deeper sense of worth and
usefulness. Likewise today God condescends to use little
people like all of us to do little jobs for him.

In Matthew 15 after the walking on the water there is a
section which may be paralleled to Acts 10 and 11. Both
passages commence with God breaking down traditional
internalistic legalism in religion. This was, and still is, a necessary prelude to effective relationship with and evangelistic outreach among Gentiles. In Acts 10 and 11 Peter's
vision convinces him that traditional laws of *kashrut* have
been overruled by God so that formerly unclean people and
animals can now be considered clean and acceptable. In the
parallel verses of Matthew 15:10–20 the disciples had to
learn that it is not what goes into the mouth which makes a
person unclean – a dangerously offensive word to Pharisees
and legalistic Christians (Mt. 15:12)! It is indeed what
comes out from the mouth and so from the heart which
shows uncleanness.

Jesus then moves to the Gentile area of Tyre and Sidon
(Mt. 15:21), thus giving opportunity for relationships with
Gentiles to develop. Matthew proceeds to tell how indeed a
Canaanite woman 'came to him' (a typical fulfilment of Old
Testament in-gathering centripetal mission). Although she
was a Gentile, she addressed him with the very Jewish title
'Lord, Son of David' which is so commonly stressed in

Matthew's Gospel. Although Jesus had taken the initiative in going to this Gentile region, he still maintains that he is 'sent only to the lost sheep of Israel' and therefore will not at first grant her request for her daughter to be healed. He is the perfect son of Abraham, Moses and David – he is the climax of Israel's history, the one perfect seed of Israel who in perfect divine holiness fulfils God's call to his people in a way which sinful Israel never could. Only when he has perfectly fulfilled God's call to Israel can he move forward to the international purposes of his Father. As it was prophesied that the Gentiles would come in to Zion, so this one individual Gentile comes to Jesus. In Acts 10 and 11 likewise the one individual Gentile, Cornelius, sends his servants to Peter and then himself comes to faith. In Matthew 15 the Canaanite woman's faith brings healing, whereas in Acts 10 and 11 Cornelius' faith led to the outpouring of the Holy Spirit as evidence that God 'accepts people from every nation' (Acts 10:35) and offers them salvation (Acts 11:14). As is well-known, Luke uses the words 'save' and 'salvation' not only for a spiritual salvation from sin and judgement, but also for a wide variety of other benefits such as physical healing and deliverance from demons.

Acts 10 and 11 with its account of the salvation in Jesus Christ of one individual Gentile leads on to the wider mission of the church both to Jews and Gentiles 'to the ends of the earth' (Acts 1:8). This movement takes a significant step forward in Antioch of Pisidia when Paul and Barnabas 'turn to the Gentiles' (Acts 13:46). Likewise in Matthew 15 the manifestation of Jesus' healing power on behalf of the Gentile woman opens the door for the feeding of a great crowd in the Gentile region 'along the sea of Galilee'. Later Jesus asked his disciples how many baskets of leftovers they had gathered after the feeding of the 5,000 and the 4,000 (Mk. 8:17–21). They replied that they had picked up twelve baskets full after the feeding of the 5,000 – twelve symbolizes Israel with its twelve tribes. And after the feeding of the 4,000 they had gathered seven baskets full – seven symbolizes perfect completion and so represents not just Israel, but *all* peoples. Jesus then said to them, 'Do you still not understand?' (Mk. 8:21). They were to be very cautious of the doubting yeast of the Pharisees and of Herod, but on the contrary should remind themselves that Jesus had fed both Jewish and Gentile crowds. This messianic sign looked forward to the ultimate eschatological table of Abraham, the messianic banquet when the Messiah would preside over a feast for all nations in his kingdom. Thus Jesus proved by his feeding of the crowds that God's kingdom had already begun on the earth, that he himself was the messianic king.

Such great claims by Jesus aroused the doubting opposition of the Pharisees and Sadducees who demanded 'a sign *from heaven*' (Mt. 16:1) – it would seem that they ignored the miraculous element in Jesus' feeding of the crowds which did demonstrate God's power in action. Jesus therefore rejects their demand and replies, 'A wicked and adulterous generation looks for a miraculous sign, but none will be given it except the sign of Jonah' (Mt. 16:4). Jesus used 'the sign of Jonah' in two ways. It sometimes refers to the three days of the death, burial and resurrection of Jesus. In Matthew 16:4 it would seem rather to point to Jonah as the one unique exception to the Old Testament rule concerning Israel's universal mission to the Gentiles. Generally Israel was not called to go out to the nations and preach God's Word to them; rather their calling, as we have seen, was to demonstrate in their life the glory, holiness and reality of God in such a way that the Gentiles would be attracted in to Zion to worship the God of Israel. But Jonah was sent out to Nineveh to preach to them – and evidently he did not enjoy his exceptional calling!

In this passage of Matthew 15:10–16:4 Jesus is therefore not only showing that he is the climax of Israel's Old Testament calling, but is also demonstrating that his heart is open for the Gentiles and is therefore preparing the ground for the church's future harvest among all nations.

The feeding of the Gentile crowd and the sign of Jonah introduce the climactic confession of Peter at Caesarea Philippi (Mt. 16:13–20): 'Who do people say the Son of Man is? . . . Who do you say I am?' And Simon Peter answers, 'You are the Messiah, the Son of the Living God,' a climactic turning point in the disciples' walk with Jesus. It is significant that this emphasis on universal mission forms the introduction to the Caesarea Philippi confession of faith in Jesus as God's Messiah. The Gospel writers unanimously point out that it is after Peter's almost credal declaration that Jesus begins to teach his disciples about his coming suffering and death.

In their 'The Biblical Foundations for Mission' Senior and Stuhlmueller demonstrate how Mark's Gospel in particular is structured around the geographical location of the ministry of Jesus. But the other Gospels reflect the same attitudes to Judea, Samaria, Galilee and the Gentile areas around the Sea of Galilee. Judea is the place of opposition and finally of crucifixion. Samaria is a way through to the Gentile world with all of its demonic opposition to Jesus' ministry among Gentiles. But in Galilee of the Gentiles Jesus feels at home, and this is where he does most of his miracles. So the geography of Jesus' ministry points to his warm-hearted love for Gentiles.

We have examined several sections of Matthew's Gospel and noted his emphasis on Jesus' positive relationship to the Gentiles. Matthew is not slow to underline Jesus' teaching that the kingdom will be taken away from those to whom it naturally adheres and that it will be given to those who were until then alien to God's kingdom. This relates particularly

in Matthew to the Gentiles, but it also applies to other
marginalized groups like leprosy sufferers, women and
children. It is from amongst the despised 'little ones' that
God will form his new people/'laos'.

But it is not only in Matthew's Gospel that we may
observe Jesus' very positive attitude to the Gentiles which
must have proved such an encouragement to the first-
century church as it battled with the general rejection of
Jesus among the Jews and as it welcomed growing numbers
of open-hearted Gentiles. Jesus' words and attitudes towards Israel and the Gentiles will have helped them to face
with confidence the violent unbelief of many Jews and the
amazing faith of so many Gentiles.

In our day too it is helpful for us to note Jesus' openness
to Samaritans and Gentiles as well as to his own Jewish
people. All who had faith in him were equally welcome.
The barriers between Jews and Gentiles were being broken
down as they came to Jesus – as also the barriers of status
between men and women, the powerful and the people of
the land, the rich and the poor. The one remaining distinction which may offend our generation is between those
who in love and faith follow Jesus and those who reject
him. Here our Lord maintained a clear distinction. Our
contemporaries today love tolerance even to the neglect of
truth, but show considerable intolerance towards anything
they consider intolerant. They may therefore appreciate
the universality of Jesus' ministry which can serve as a
model for us as we seek to remove all status symbols in the
church and in society, all barriers of race, class, gender or
generation. But they may dislike the particularity of Jesus'
relationships in which repentance and faith in Jesus the
Messiah and Lord are a precondition for entry into his
kingdom.

Luke also emphasizes Jesus' relationship towards the
Gentiles. Having served for a while as a missionary

companion to Paul, the apostle to the Gentiles, it is hardly surprising that Paul's convictions concerning universal mission influenced Luke. Luke's emphasis on Jesus' concern for Gentiles is such a marked characteristic both of the book of Acts and of Luke's gospel, that many scholars consider that Luke was himself a Gentile, indeed the only Gentile author in the Bible. I personally doubt this, but the question is not relevant to our discussion in this book. It makes little difference whether Luke gained his interest only from the life of Jesus himself and from his experience with Paul or whether it also stems from his own ethnic background.

The structure of the book of Acts is reflected also in Luke's gospel. In Acts, as we have already indicated, chapters 1–7 relate to mission among Jews; Acts 8 has the two-fold bridge between Jews and Gentiles, namely the Samaritans and the Ethiopian eunuch; then in Acts 9 the story of the wider mission to all peoples has its beginning. Likewise Luke's gospel commences with three very Jewish chapters which have an almost Old Testament character. The songs of Mary, Zechariah, the angels and Simeon could easily have fitted into the pages of the Old Testament. So too the various characters who appear on the stage in Luke 1–3 are all very Jewish. The emphasis on the Temple in these chapters is also significant – it is noteworthy that the gospel returns to the Temple as its conclusion (Lk. 24:53). Despite the wider outlook in his gospel Luke still has the life of Jesus in his incarnate ministry based in the Temple, the locus of God's presence and therefore of the praise of God.

We have already observed Luke's emphasis on the Gentiles right from the outset of Jesus' ministry in Luke 4. We saw how his 'words of grace' (4:32) applied not only to Jesus' concern for the poor, the prisoners, the blind and the oppressed, but also for the Gentiles. The sequel to the Nazareth synagogue reading recounts Jesus' positive words showing that already in the days of Elijah and

Elisha God's gracious mercy extended to the widow in Zarephath and to Naaman the Syrian. Thus Jesus shows that his ministry is not in the matter of the Gentiles radically new, but is in direct continuity with God's working in the Old Testament.

As in his Acts of the Apostles, so also in his gospel Luke has a bridge between the Jewish and Gentile sections. In his Gospel that bridge is the genealogy of Jesus (Lk. 3:23–28). In Matthew's Gospel the genealogy fits appropriately as the very first verses introducing the whole book. Matthew's Gospel is written to show that despite all that was happening in Matthew's time Christians could still be confident that Jesus really was Israel's Messiah and saviour. The genealogy shows how Jesus is the true son of David and of Abraham. But Luke's genealogy relates more widely than just to Israel. Jesus is the son of Adam, the father of all humanity. And Adam is the son of God, so God's purpose is to be the father of all peoples. All nations can be and should be God's children. This universal emphasis does not entirely fit Luke 1–3, but is an appropriate introduction to Jesus' ministry which will also include Gentiles. Actually Luke 1–3 already hints at this more universal element of Jesus' concerns. These first chapters are like a prelude to a great piece of music; the major themes are already touched upon in the introductory music. So the Jewish reader may wonder who is referred to as 'those living in darkness and in the shadow of death' (Lk. 1:79), but quickly returns to the assurance that "God will guide *our* feet into the path of peace.' Simeon's song is more definite in declaring that God's salvation is for 'all people, a light for revelation to the Gentiles', but here too the reader is quickly brought back to the Jewish people by the words 'and for glory to your people Israel' (Lk. 2:31,32). With reference to John the Baptist Luke quotes Isaiah that 'all mankind will see God's salvation' (Lk. 3:6) and John in his preaching declares that God can raise up children of Abraham even out of stones – Israel cannot count on the exclusive position of being the elect children of Abraham.

So Luke underlines the universal ministry of Jesus. Jesus is not narrow or exclusive in his relationships, but is concerned for Jews and Gentiles alike.

John's gospel

We have already seen in our brief study of John 4 that in John's gospel Jesus extends the borders of the kingdom of God to include a sinful Samaritan woman. As the good shepherd Jesus has 'other sheep that are not of this sheep pen' (Jn. 10:16). He feels within himself an obligation to bring them also under his care. With confidence he asserts that 'they too will listen to my voice' with the result that Jews and Gentiles together will form 'one flock' under 'one shepherd'. Jesus so loves the universal flock of sheep that he 'lays down his life for the sheep' (10:11, 15, 17, 18) – the repeated words underline Jesus' sacrificial love for the sake of his followers.

John's gospel contains a series of visible signs with an accompanying word to elucidate the significance of the sign. As is common in the New Testament (e.g. Matthew and Luke/Acts) sign and word go hand in hand – a model for mission throughout the ages. The series of signs in the first half of the gospel (Jn. 1–12) introduces the climactic final sign of the death and resurrection of Jesus. As in the other gospels, Jesus' death and resurrection hold centre stage as the ultimate and essential purpose of Jesus' incarnate life on earth. To demonstrate the vital importance of his death and resurrection as God's final sign, John sandwiches the word between two sections of the sign. So Jesus' final great word in John 14–17 is bracketed by the washing of the disciples' feet which introduces Jesus' great sacrifice on the cross.

But what is the last sign in the introductory John 1–12 which opens the way to the climactic sign of the cross and the empty tomb? It is the coming of the Greeks (not Hellenists, as some scholars have suggested) to see Jesus (Jn. 12:20ff). They did not go directly to Jesus, but first approached Philip, who had a Greek, not a Jewish, name. John significantly adds the explanation that Philip 'was from Bethsaida in Galilee' (a largely Gentile area). Perhaps Philip remembered Jesus' hesitation in receiving the Gentile Canaanite woman, but that is only speculation. But we are told that for one reason or another Philip informed Andrew of the Greeks' request and together they went to tell Jesus.

R.E. Brown in the Anchor Bible Commentary on John's gospel comments, 'only the understanding that the first Gentiles have come to Jesus explains his exclamation that the hour has come'. Whether in fact these were the *first* Gentiles to come to Jesus is debatable – did not the wise men from the east, the Roman centurion (Mt. 8:5) and the Canaanite woman come to Jesus before the Greeks? But certainly that coming is seen by John and evidently by Jesus himself as a fulfilment of the Old Testament which, as Brown says, 'indicates that it is time for him to lay down his life'. The other sheep which are not of the Jewish sheep pen have begun to come to Jesus. Jesus is therefore excitedly aware that his hour has come to be glorified; now he can move forward to the cross where he will be lifted up and draw to himself 'all people' (Jn. 12:32), not just the people of Israel.

As we have already noted, the Old Testament calling of Israel was so to live in the holiness of God that the nations would be attracted to Israel and its focal point in the Temple where God dwelt. Jesus sees himself as the perfect Israelite whose life not only reflects God's holiness, but actually is the very image of God in absolute holiness. Now the Gentiles are to come to Jesus, who subsumes within his own being all that Israel, their land and its central point, the Temple, were called to be. Therefore the coming of the Gentile Greeks to Jesus stirs his emotions and he responds excitedly (Jn. 12:23ff).

We note therefore that Jesus' heartfelt motive in his crucifixion specifically includes eternal life also for the Gentiles. This loving purpose in the heart of God is apparent already in the very first chapter of John's gospel. It is often said that the Prologue to John's gospel (Jn. 1:1–18) gives a summary of all that the rest of John's gospel will expound. The Prologue is John's gospel in a nutshell. Let us therefore look at John 1 to see Jesus' relationship to the Gentiles.

From early in Christian history these verses have been expounded primarily to prove that the incarnate second person of the Trinity was both fully divine and fully human, but it is doubtful whether this Greek debate was in the forefront of Jewish John's mind. Although the theological truth of the divine-humanity of Christ is clearly present in the first verses of the Prologue, it is not John's primary concern. His overriding concern is to show that Christ, the Word of God, is the creator and was 'with god' in the act of creation.

So the Prologue begins with a reiterated emphasis that the Word was God's instrument of creation 'in the beginning' (Gen. 1:1, Jn. 1:1,3). In the Old Testament the fact of creation is commonly used to undergird God's claim that all creation and all people belong to him (e.g. 2 Kgs. 19:5, Psa. 24:1–2). So too in John 1:3 the words 'all things' and 'nothing' underline the universality of God's purposes in Christ. Indeed the word 'all' together with 'many' and 'much' is an oft-repeated key word through John's gospel.

John proceeds to show that in the Word was the life which is the light not just of Israel, but of all people. This light shines in the darkness. This faces the reader with the question: what or who is 'the darkness'? The darkness is clearly the world which is outside of God's covenanted grace, indeed particularly the Gentile world. This emphasis on the universality of God's purposes in Christ is again repeated in John 1:7 and 9. His purpose is that 'all people might believe' and to this end the true light, Jesus Christ, 'who gives light to everybody was coming into the world' (Jn. 1:9). The word 'world' appears four times in quick succession in the context of the creation ('the world was made through him') and thus of universality. Why does John draw such particular attention to the word 'the world'?

Although the context is clearly that 'the world was made through him' (1:10), John's readers would have known that the story of creation in Genesis 1 and 2 nowhere says that God created the world. The word used in Genesis is 'the earth'. The Hebrew word for 'earth', *erets*, is commonly associated with 'the land of Israel' – *erets Israel* – and that is precisely what John does not want to say. So he carefully changes from the particularistic 'erets' to the definitely universalistic 'kosmos' and repeats the word four times to ensure that his readers note the importance of the word. Jesus Christ is not only in relationship with the land and people of Israel, but with the totality of 'the world'. Sadly however 'the world did not recognize him' and the Roman Gentiles joined with the Jews in crucifying him.

It was not just the Gentiles who rejected Jesus; John proceeds to tell the tragic fact that Jesus came to his own (Jewish people), but 'his own did not receive him' (Jn. 1:11). The repetition of 'his own' underlines the heartrending pathos of Israel's refusal to accept Jesus as Messiah and Lord.

Happily the sad realities both of Gentile and Jewish rejection of Jesus are followed by the positive grace of 1:12, 13. This grace is given 'to all who received him, to those who believed in his name'. The precondition is clear – it is for those who do not reject Jesus, but accept and receive him into their lives; it is for those who entrust themselves to him as 'Jesus'/saviour. The universality of Jesus' saving grace is further evidenced by this statement that it is for *all* who receive and believe in him. We have already noted that in John's gospel 'all' refers particularly to the Gentiles. To them Jesus has given 'the right to become children of God'. In the Old Testament Israel was given the gracious privilege of being God's children (e.g. Ex. 4:22, Jer. 31:9, Hos. 11:1), but through faith in Jesus Christ the Gentiles can also now become God's children. John does not merely say that they can 'be' God's children like Israel, but that they can 'become' what they were not before. The meaning of this is further explained in the following verse (Jn. 1:13). Gentiles who are in a vital relationship with Jesus by faith are 'born of God', not 'of natural descent'. Adoption into God's family as brothers and sisters of Jesus Christ does not depend on being the blood children of Abraham, Isaac and Jacob. It is not an ethnic issue; it is a question of faith in Jesus Christ.

So John underlines Jesus' relationship also to Gentiles. The Word which reveals God's glory, grace and truth has not only become a first-century Jew in a particularistic manner, but has in a more universal sense 'become flesh' (1:14). So Jesus in his messianic ministry of life and salvation invites and welcomes both Jews and Gentiles into his kingdom, into relationship with himself and with his Father.

From this New Testament emphasis on Jesus' universalistic relationships we are compelled to draw two fundamental conclusions.

Firstly, the ministry of Jesus breaks down all ethnic and other barriers within the body of his followers. The church of God dare not allow racial prejudice or narrow ethnic pride (or any other status distinction which is divisive). Paul realized the vital significance of this when he declared that all who are children of God through faith in Jesus Christ are now one in equality – Jews and Gentiles, slaves and free, men and women (Gal. 3:26–28).

Secondly, Jesus wants people of all backgrounds to come into relationship with him. Therefore as his servants we are called to pray and work in his mission to all people everywhere. Worldwide mission is not an optional extra for the Christian church; it is essential if we are to relate to Christ and share his mind and heart.

What then lies at the heart of Jesus' relationships eschatologically? What therefore do we as his people eagerly look forward to and strive for? There will be 'a great multitude from every nation, tribe, people and language standing before the throne and in front of the Lamb' (Rev. 7:9), falling on our faces in worship. He is the universal Lord who opens his heart for loving relationships with everyone on earth: Jew, Samaritan, Gentile, old or young, rich or poor. We unite in worshipping him. To his name be all the glory.